MARGARET THATCHER

A PERSONAL AND POLITICAL BIOGRAPHY

RUSSELL LEWIS

ROUTLEDGE & KEGAN PAUL
LONDON AND BOSTON

First published in 1975
by Routledge & Kegan Paul Ltd
Broadway House, 68– 74 Carter Lane,
London EC4V 5EL and
9 Park Street,
Boston, Mass. 02108, USA
Set in 11/14 pt Baskerville by Autoset, Brentwood,
and printed in Great Britain by
The Camelot Press Ltd, Southampton

ISBN 0 7100 8283 5

To Oliver, Martin and Daniel

CONTENTS

PLATES

Between pages 20-21, 116-117 and 148-149

Eastern Approaches, 1972 (*Daily Telegraph*)
In command—after three years as Minister, 1973 (*Daily Telegraph*)
Mrs 9½ per cent, 1974 (*Daily Telegraph*)
In the boudoir, 1974 (Sun London)
Politics in the family, 1975 (Sun London)
Foot in the door—after the first ballot, 1975 (*Daily Telegraph*)
Sweet smile of success, 1975 (*Guardian*)
Thatchers triumphant, 1975 (Syndication International)
Brief Encounter—with Mr Whitelaw, 1975 (Popperfoto)
Study of the victor, 1975 (Fox)
Just for the record—with Jimmy Young, 1975 (*Daily Telegraph*)
Three for Europe—with the President and Secretary General of the European Parliament, 1975 (Popperfoto)
Leading Lady, 1975 (Press Association)
Off the cuff with Reagan, 1975 (Press Association)
Answers for well-wishers, 1975 (*Daily Telegraph*)
'Looking like a new pin', 1975 (*Sunday Telegraph*)
With Pierre Trudeau, 1975 (Central Press)
At the Elysée—with President Giscard d'Estaing, 1975 (Popperfoto)
'My husband's in oil', 1975 (Central Press)
United for Europe, 1975 (Central Press)
Ideal Home, 1975 (Central Press)

PREFACE
AND
ACKNOWLEDGMENTS

I should like to thank the many who have helped and advised me in what had to be the rapid composition and production of this book. In particular I should mention Mr Tom Bourne the Conservative agent in Grantham; Mrs Margaret Wickstead of Lincoln and Miss D.M. O'Donnell, Bursar of Somerville College, Oxford; various old colleagues at Conservative Central Office and especially Mrs Pamela Leger, head of the press cuttings department; Mr Derek Howe, Mrs Thatcher's press officer; Mr George Hutchinson and Dr Rhodes Boyson. I am especially grateful to Mrs Gay Lewis, who brilliantly and quickly translated my manuscript into type. I am also beholden to Routledge & Kegan Paul for producing the book so nicely in spite of the haste, and in particular to Mr Timothy O'Sullivan for editorial help and suggesting that I write the book in the first place. Naturally they have had no part in any errors I may have committed, for which all blame must attach to myself.

The cartoons on pages 110-11 and 130-1 appear by permission of the *Daily Express* and *Spectator* respectively.

Finally may I say in anticipation to all who buy this book, and purloining a phrase attributed to Mr Tony Benn, 'It's a pleasure to have your company'.

Russell Lewis

1

A STAR IS BORN

There is a tide in the affairs not only of men but of women too, which, taken at the flood, leads on to fortune. And flood tide for Margaret Hilda Thatcher was not when she finally triumphed in the second ballot for the Conservative Party leadership: it was when she decided that, come what may, she would make her challenge to the old leader—Edward Heath. Mr Enoch Powell was to say later that she was merely lucky: that she happened to be in the right place at the right time. Yet, as Mr Powell has said in a graphic account of another, earlier leadership struggle, Mr (now Lord) R. A. Butler was also in the right place at the right time. The difference was that when the revolver was loaded and placed in his hand he could not bring himself to pull the trigger. The story of Mrs Thatcher's life seems in retrospect to have been evolving towards this moment of truth, and, even if this be dismissed as a biographer's fond illusion, yet certainly the study of her life and career makes it no matter of surprise that when opportunity knocked she, unlike R.A. Butler, had her hand on the latch.

For the British public the first full realisation that a new star had appeared in the political firmament was on Tuesday, 4

February 1975. Few who were present will quickly forget the air of excitement when the count was announced. As MPs and others pressed into room 14 of the House of Commons the voting totals were read out—Edward Heath 119, Margaret Thatcher 130, Hugh Fraser 16. The figures were truly astounding. Nothing in the press had prepared anyone for any such result. The editorials had generally pronounced Mr Heath preferable to Mrs Thatcher (with the honourable exceptions of the *Daily Mail* and the *Spectator*). The lobby correspondents, pontificating on the basis of their special knowledge, had confidently predicted a Heath gain, and Ladbroke's were giving odds on Mr Heath and odds against Mrs Thatcher. *The Economist* appeared to sum up for the higher journalism, when it called for a quick and decisive victory for Mr Heath. The only worry seemed to be that Mrs Thatcher might prevent his getting the required margin for an outright win, thus holding out the irksome prospect of a further ballot with new hats galore being flung into the ring.

Besides, had not the public opinion polls—especially the last *Daily Express* poll of party supporters—shown Mr Heath out in front? Had not the census of supporters' opinion in the constituencies, carefully taken by the Conservative voluntary organisation, the National Union, come up with formidable statistics of the grass roots rooting for Ted? Had not the Peers too overwhelmingly expressed their preference for no change, as did the trendy Young Conservatives of the Greater London area and the top men of the Tory leadership—Lord Carrington, Mr Willie Whitelaw, even Sir Alec Douglas Home, not to mention retired grandees like Tony (now Lord) Barber, who emerged briefly from the portals of his city bank to back his old chief. How strange then, when, seemingly, all that was venerable and progressive, old and young, sophisticated and innocent, mighty and modest in the Tory party was united to save Mr Heath from political extinction, extinguished he was—at the hands of a comparative unknown, and what is more a woman!

Yet the signs were there, if people had wanted to read them. As one senior party official said to the author afterwards, 'What those clever, but inexperienced, youngsters in the Heath private office failed to appreciate was the elementary fact that the MPs did decide to have an election for Leader—well then why should they have an election for a new Leader, if all they wanted to do was to keep the old one? It would have been a waste of time. The whole point of having an election was to elect somebody else.'

Why did they want a change? Partly it was their gut feeling that Mr Heath, for all his many qualities, was a born loser. He had lost three elections out of the four in his time as Leader, and his form was not improving. He was showing an increasing preference in his choice of confidantes and advisers for those who fell in with his views or who were ill qualified on grounds of either seniority, experience or qualification to disagree with him, so that he could trample on them with ease. It was a striking fact that his *bêtes noires* among Conservative-minded journalists included some of the most able people in Fleet Street. Perhaps, as a result of his lone early struggle he had become too proud to be beholden to anyone. He appeared to believe that, by sheer determination, he had won the 1970 election all on his own. So it was that in Government, guided by his own imperious will, impatient with industrialists for whom he had such profound contempt (because they would not invest even when he offered them the most advantageous allowances) and confident that he could wear down by sheer psychological attrition any resistance from the unions, he would single-handed make the British economy prosper and grow. And, with the prosperity and growth he could buy all the doubters and the faint hearts and even obdurate back-woodsmen who wanted no part of the chromium-plated modernised Britain with which he yearned to present them.

In the last analysis, it was this pride, this illusion of

independence (which dwelt strangely in a man who had given so much of his political energies to proving that no country, let alone individual, could be a sovereign island in the modern world) which was the source of his downfall. The cynics were wrong who said it was just a matter of the Tories ruthlessly eliminating the man who had brought them to defeat. They could have forgiven failure if Mr Heath had inspired their affection as well as their respect, and political life has a cruel way of bringing such lessons home. Suddenly the man who wanted to do it all himself was left to his own devices. When he resigned from the leadership, out of all the Shadows, only Lord Carrington, one of nature's gentlemen, went round to his old chief to express his consolation and regrets.

It would be churlish to dwell further on the vices of the vanquished, and unenlightening if it should lead us to forget the virtues of the victor. Yet the strange fact is that, until the leadership struggle, or at least until the October 1975 election, in which she played a leading role, Mrs Thatcher was comparatively unknown. Indeed, in the immediate aftermath of that election, when the discussion of a possible successor for Heath began, her name was scarcely considered. For that matter, she dismissed the idea herself. The Conservatives were not prepared yet to have a woman as Leader, she said. How then did she rise to first place so swiftly? The simple luck theory will only take us so far. Margaret Thatcher's main stroke of luck was that fate had removed those who might have been preferred on grounds of seniority or experience or even sex. No one could have been more conscious of this than Mr Enoch Powell himself. It was he who, so he would argue, had brought about the destruction of Mr Heath. Yet, even if we accept for a moment this arguable contention, it is clear that his manner of doing it—by calling upon his erstwhile supporters, not in one, but in two, elections running, to vote Labour, and then crossing the Irish channel to return in the bizarre guise of an Ulster Loyalist, had plainly disqualified him from participating in the

Tory leadership stakes.

Of more immediate importance was the decision of Sir Keith Joseph to back down. He had been a leading contender and Mrs Thatcher had been his staunch ally. It was Sir Keith who set things in motion, even before the October election, by his speech—*The Times* even gave a whole page to it—that he and his colleagues in the Conservative Cabinet had been collectively wrong in failing to make the defeat of inflation their first priority. He also blamed his colleagues and himself for recklessly expanding the money supply (in pursuit of full employment and growth) because this only made inflation worse.

It is to be hoped that Sir Keith's thoughtful speeches helped to enlighten the British public: what is more certain is that they undermined the complacency with which many Conservatives still viewed their own record in power. Unfortunately a curious slip of taste or judgment, at least in presentation, led Sir Keith to reflect publicly on the probable need to issue free contraceptives in order to reduce the number of unwanted children borne by subnormal, unmarried working-class mothers. The furore which this caused, and the loss of nerve which Sir Keith showed in trying to rebut it (thereby ignoring Disraeli's famous advice 'Never apologise, never retract'), put out of the race the one man that Mrs Thatcher definitely would not stand against. Still, Sir Keith had really done Mrs Thatcher's hatchet work for her, and here it should be noted that he and she were politically more than just friends: they were extremely close allies. They had found their views converging in the Heath Cabinet, and after the February 1974 electoral defeat they would only join the Shadow Cabinet on condition that they were able to start up their own research establishment with Party financial support. This was the so-called 'Centre for Policy Studies' in Wilfred Street, of which Sir Keith and Margaret became Vice Presidents and which was intended to expound and develop the idea of a 'social market economy', as originally expounded by Professor Erhardt, and which, when put into practice, resulted in West Germany's post-war economic miracle. In any event, when Sir Keith stepped down, Margaret Thatcher stepped forward.

It was widely believed that Edward Du Cann, Chairman of the 1922 Committee of Tory back-benchers, would throw his hat in the ring. In the event though, the decisive voice seems to have been that of his wife Sally, who (in this respect, like Sir Keith's wife) counselled against it.

At the same time the decision of Ted Heath not to stand aside in favour of Mr Willie Whitelaw—the favourite of the Heath faction—made it certain that no Heath supporter other than Mr Heath himself, would stand. So, by a process of elimination, the only serious contender against Mr Heath in the first ballot was Mrs Margaret Thatcher. It also happened that, just when she needed them, Mr Airey Neave and a number of other Tory MPs who were keen to remove Mr Heath discovered that she had no organisation and came eagerly forward to supply it. Mr Airey Neave is an unusual man. He had gained fame for escaping from Colditz during the war and then, as if that was not enough, became escape organiser for MI9. At this stage he had been on the back benches for over fifteen years—since 1959 in fact, when he left office in the Macmillan Government owing to a minor heart condition. Apparently, after seeing his doctor, who told him to rest, he went to see Mr Heath, who was then Mr Macmillan's Chief Whip, and explained that he would regrettably have to resign. 'Well that's the end of your political career', said Mr Heath brutally. Since then Mr Heath had gone on to become Prime Minister while Mr Neave had retreated to the back benches and had apparently reached the end of his political career as his leader had surmised. Yet, as the title of Mr Neave's book on his wartime experiences put it, 'They have their exits', and in the end it fell to him to show Mr Heath the way out.

Yet, if fate was kind to Margaret Thatcher in removing rivals and providing the right allies at the right time, nothing would be more unwise than to attribute the Thatcher triumph to that alone, for it needed a certain firmness of mind and character to grasp the opportunity thus presented, and no one who has met Mrs Thatcher has ever doubted that here is a lady of determined will. She also has other more appealing qualities. It is a good start that Mrs Thatcher, who is 50 this year, is an attractive woman with a stylish dress sense—she once modelled tweed suits for the *Daily Telegraph.*

From the point of view of the Fleet Street women's editors, her sudden rise to the top is the most interesting development since Twiggy, but more substantial. She combines feminine elegance with a mind which delights in legal and statistical complexities. She has an incisive manner of speaking, happily free from umms and ers, and, perhaps, a tribute to the elocution lessons she took while still a young girl. She can be imperious, but she remains feminine and, if sometimes rather sharp, her manner remains gracious. Her arrival at the head of the Conservative Party in this country is something of a bombshell. Is she a nine-day wonder, or does she constitute a new, indeed revolutionary, phenomenon in British political life? She certainly talks the language and shares the fears and aspirations of the grass-roots Tories. She really believes, but with unusual vehemence and passion, that law-breakers and vandals should be punished and not treated as folk heroes; that those who work and save should have their just reward, that competition and free enterprise, not controls and bureaucracy, are the means to prosperity, that government should practise economy, and that the great evil of inflation is largely the result of government extravagance and waste. Of course the Left have tried to foist on her the image of a limited suburban reactionary—it would be more true to say that her views are rather commonplace. She is altogether too representative of the gut feeling in the constituencies to suit many of the Gurus of the Fleet Street establishment. This is no doubt what she herself means when she talks, as she frequently has, of being an ordinary woman, leading Lynda Lee Potter, in an article in the *Daily Mail*, to cry out in exasperation, 'I do wish she would stop going on about how damned ordinary she is'. Miss Lee Potter should not worry. Mrs Thatcher belongs within a great tradition: she has common views, but uncommon abilities. If she seems to some off-puttingly like a paragon, at least she is a paragon with her feet on the ground, and if her appearance at the front of the political stage seemed sudden, surprising and even alarming, she did not exactly spring fully armed into the world, like Athene from the head of Zeus: like most Conservative leaders, she emerged, but by what manner is what the ensuing pages are largely about.

2

GRANTHAM AND OXFORD

The theme 'From log cabin to White House' dominates American folklore. Yet the tradition is not so much American as Anglo-Saxon, for throughout British history too, talented and energetic individuals of humble birth have scaled the heights of fortune and success. Not least among those was Margaret R. rts, the future leader of the Conservative Party. She was born on 13 October 1925, the second daughter of unpretentious parents in a small provincial town. Her father was a grocer who had left school at the age of 12 and her mother had been a dressmaker. One of her grandfathers had been a shoemaker, the other a railway guard. Grantham, the town of her birth, which even now numbers only 28,000 inhabitants, is still one of the few genuinely old English towns to have survived the assaults of both the commercial developer and the municipal vandal. In 1963 it was to celebrate its five hundredth anniversary as a borough. Yet the splendour of its parish church, which when it was built circa 1300 had the highest spire in Britain, is evidence of the town's prosperity even in the high Middle Ages, and much earlier it was important enough for King John to hold court there at the Angel Inn. The grammar school founded by Edward IV has the claim to glory that it educated Isaac Newton. The eye is also caught by William Watkin's Town Hall, topped as it is by an almost comically large clock lantern which might have been designed to arouse the protective instincts of Sir John Betjeman. These are landmarks which stand out in an urban landscape which is for the most part pleasingly spacious because the streets are wide and the roofs are low, and there are many old houses in Georgian brick and, older still, in stone, most of them displaying large, comfortable-looking, white-painted windows.

The grocer's shop on the corner over which Margaret lived for her first eighteen years became a rather larger affair than is indicated by recent photographs in the press, because the premises have now been divided into two, one half being a sub-Post Office, the other an antique shop. Yet, if it became quite a solid business which employed five assistants, it did not allow any frills. In the family flat over the shop there was no bath and no hot running water. The family was, according to one friend's later account, 'Never rich, never poor'. Riches or deprivation are, however, comparative and for Grantham the inter-war period was economically far from being its finest hour. The Depression had struck at both farming and heavy engineering and Grantham, as a market town and a centre of steam locomotive and diesel manufacture, was doubly unfortunate. Indeed the town's main employer, Ruston and Hornsby, which in the Great War had plunged into armaments, found, when peace came, that demand had collapsed and duly went broke, throwing many Grantham people out of work.

Alfred Roberts was a prominent Rotarian and a leading citizen. He had a commanding presence, helped by the fact that he was about 6 ft 2 in. tall. According to the local librarian he was the best-read man in Grantham and Margaret collected armfuls of books for him every week, his special interests being current affairs and the Welfare State. Like many self-educated men he had a certain do-it-yourself incisiveness, and, from all accounts, an unusual capacity for getting to an argument's heart—qualities which he seems to have passed on to his younger daughter, Margaret. He was a staunch Methodist, a lay preacher, a teetotaller and, taking his family with him, a three-times-on-Sunday chapel attender. According to the local newsagent, he never took a Sunday newspaper. Elsewhere his sort of person often became a leading light in the Labour Party, but Alfred Roberts was, if anything, a Liberal. In any case, when he joined the council two years after his second daughter was born, it was at the behest of his fellow members of the Chamber of Trade, and as an Independent. He served on Grantham Council for twenty-five years with particular distinction—as Chairman of the Finance Committee. He rose to become Mayor and continued to serve thereafter as an Alderman. Rather shabbily, in 1952 Labour claimed back his Aldermanic seat and sacked him from the Council. He, however, accepted the situation with impressive dignity and restraint. He laid down his robes and said, just audibly and, to those present, movingly, 'No medals, no honours, but an inward sense of satisfaction. May God bless Grantham forever.'

Margaret showed ability early and at the Huntingtower Road Elementary School she was immediately put into a class for children a year older than herself. There was a story that, at the age of 9, she won a poetry reading prize at a local drama festival. Her headmistress said, 'You were lucky Margaret!' to which Margaret replied, 'I wasn't lucky, I deserved it.' At the age of 10, a year younger than was normal, she easily passed the scholarship examination and went to the Kesteven and Grantham Girls' Grammar School, where she always worked hard, and where she failed to come top in only one of the seven years of her school career. One of her schoolmates was Margaret Goodrich, who later on was to go up to Lady Margaret Hall in Oxford at the same time that Margaret Roberts went to Somerville. She says that Margaret was determined from a very early age to become a Member of Parliament. Her first memory of Margaret Roberts was of a little fair-haired girl from Form Two confidently standing up, with enormous self-assurance, to ask the speaker (who as it happened was Bernard Newman, the famous authority on spies) a question—not really the sort of thing that girls from Form Two did! Margaret Roberts was not only good at her work, but good at practically everything else, including games—she played centre half in the school hockey team—and took part in theatricals. Margaret never wavered in her determination to get on, and the way forward was through Oxford. At that time entry to Oxford University was far more difficult for a girl than a boy because there were few women's colleges and therefore fewer places. As she was good at all subjects she seems to have decided rather coolly and calculatingly that for a girl Chemistry was the best examination bet. There was also the attraction of invading and succeeding in what was considered a man's domain. This trait was to reappear later in her political career, when she deliberately tried to keep clear of the women's territory, like the social services, and to make her name in the 'male' subjects of public finance and taxation. Even a scientist, however, could not go to Oxford without achieving a certain standard in Latin. So, for a fee, Margaret was crammed for two terms. Yet Miss Gillies, the headmistress, apparently wanted Margaret to wait until her third year before she took the Oxford entrance. There was, perhaps, just a slight feeling, once common among grammar school teachers, that those of their pupils who set their sights on the older universities were getting a bit above themselves. In any case, Margaret was hopping mad. 'She's trying to thwart my ambition', she said, and though in the end Margaret *did* take the exam, this episode appears to have left a strong resentment. Years later, when she came back to speak at a school celebration and was preceded by Miss Gillies (now retired) who quoted some Latin tag, Mrs Thatcher uncharitably and rather uncharacteristically corrected her, which was not liked by the audience, few of whom could have known how much that early attempt to thwart her ambition had rankled.

At this time Margaret Goodrich's father, the vicar at Coleby (where he had what was considered the nicest vicarage in the diocese), took a kindly interest and offered to help Margaret Roberts obtain a place at Nottingham. In the event Margaret did make Somerville (Oxford) after all. She had already been nominated Head Girl, but held the position for only a fortnight. Her name went up on the plaque none the less, and if there had been any doubt about it the matter was probably clinched by the fact that Alfred Roberts was the Chairman of the school's Board of Governors. The school's roll of honour also gives the names of girls who won university degrees. Mostly there were only one or two for the year. One big exception however was 1945, Margaret's year, for then there were six—an unusually good crop of brains, certainly, but also surely a tribute to the value of competition!

The picture of Margaret Roberts that appears so far is perhaps rather alarming: this fiercely determined young girl pressing forward ruthlessly towards the fulfilment of her ambitions, apparently untouched by the usual childish naughtiness. Yet the fact is she had a very full life at school, helped to serve in the shop, learnt to play the piano, took elocution lessons and read omnivorously. In any case, it was wartime. Restrictions were many, distractions were few. Besides there was always plenty of interest in what her father was doing, for he was at the centre of anything of consequence going on in the town. He was on the Bench too, and it was through him that Margaret was able to meet leading people at the Bar. One of them, the Recorder, Norman Winning, who turned out to have a Physics degree from Cambridge, advised her one day at lunch to continue her studies in science if she wanted eventually to go on in the law, for a scientific background might help her to specialise lucratively in patent law. Reading about all these mature manoeuvrings, it is easy to overlook the reality that, as her friend Margaret Goodrich (now

Mrs Wickstead) has said, she had, and still has, a very soft and generous side to her nature. When she came to tea at the vicarage at Coleby she never forgot to bring some butter. Margaret's elder sister, Muriel, who might quite naturally have been expected to resent her for being such a goodie at school, especially when the teachers made unfavourable comparisons, became incensed years later at the suggestion that Margaret was cold and aloof. Muriel (by that time Mrs Cullen) told a *Daily Telegraph* reporter, just before the second ballot result, that Margaret was 'a warm and very generous person, and someone who is genuinely interested in other people'. Certainly an upbringing in a small well knit community can not only make for a stability and strength of character, it also breeds the friendlier, kindlier, gentler qualities. On becoming Conservative leader, Margaret wrote a special message to the *Grantham Journal,* in which she said, 'I always believe that I was very lucky to have been brought up in a small town with a great sense of friendliness and voluntary service.'

Yet small communities can also be limiting and oppressive. Oxford now beckoned, and though Oxford was also in a sense a closed society, with its own powerful conformities, to the intellectually adventurous and the ambitious it was the gateway to a wider world. Somerville, to which Margaret had obtained entrance, was, along with Lady Margaret Hall, the first women's college in Oxford when it was founded in 1879. Women, however, had a struggle to be admitted to university degrees and it was not until 1920 that they were made full members of the University. The college has produced more than its quota of leading politicians, including (in addition to Mrs Thatcher) Mrs Indira Ghandi, Dr Edith Summerskill and Mrs Shirley Williams who, it is quite on the cards, may become leader of the British Labour Party. The Principal when Margaret went up there was Dame Janet Vaughan, who is famous for her work on bone structure and radiation effects. Yet intellectually the most distinguished product of Somerville was Margaret's teacher, Dorothy Hodgkin, who has since won the Nobel Prize for Chemistry, and is the first British woman since Florence Nightingale to receive the Order of Merit. It was still wartime when Margaret went up but, in the latter part of her time, the war over, the bulk of the undergraduates were ex-service people and they made it to a greater extent than before and probably since a democratic Oxford—everybody was on a par because everybody was on a grant. One contemporary suggested that three recent British leaders, Mr Wilson, Mr Heath and Mrs Thatcher, had all been formed by their reaction to Oxford, and that their reaction was an unfavourable one. For all three were clever young people of petty middle-class origin, who were dumped in what was still a playground of the British upper middle-class, and their response was a certain edginess, an ultimate lack of confidence which manifested itself later in life, especially in irritation with criticism and meanness with the press. The formula is a little too neat, for the ex-service Oxford Margaret knew was, because of the ex-service element, less class conscious than the Oxford of the 1930s attended by Messrs Heath and Wilson. Besides, for a pretty girl class barriers tend to disappear, and she has never had any problems of being shy with people.

Margaret was a serious girl and had little time for frivolities. The chemistry students had less time for play than the arts people in any case, because they had to spend their afternoons in the laboratories, and that is one reason why science students generally play less part in Oxford's extra-mural activities even today. Despite this, Margaret managed to shine politically, not in the prestigious Union Society (which held regular debates) which women were still not allowed to join, but in the University Conservative Club (OUCA) of which she became Chairman in 1946. It was an exciting time in politics. The Socialists were in power in Westminster but, as often happens, the students were moving in the opposite direction. She did not have a large circle of friends, but one of the friends she met, through politics, was Sir Edward Boyle, who preceded her as Chairman of the University Conservatives and was also President of the Union. Her sister, Muriel, remembers how she went up to see Margaret and was taken to the Union Society where she heard Wedgwood Benn speaking. 'Today I often think', she told the *Daily Mail*, 'It is all very well for him to attack class and privilege, but he didn't have to struggle, nor did his children, with the enormous trust funds his wife's family set up for them.'

Margaret graduated, taking a second class honours, which, incidentally, would in other universities be called an upper second. A friend remembers her saying, 'I wish I'd never done chemistry. I never thought I'd get a first: I spent too much time on politics.' 'She was a perfectly competent and ordinary young woman,' Dame Janet Vaughan, Somerville's Principal, recalled. Dame Janet was no doubt thinking of her skill as a chemist, in which she was evidently competent and which provided her with her first job as research chemist at BX Plastics where she studied surface tensions. Yet, as time was to reveal, her political gifts were far from ordinary. She went to live in Manningtree in Essex, where she joined the local Conservatives and did some speaking. As it happened, things were to move more quickly on this side of her life than she had any right to expect.

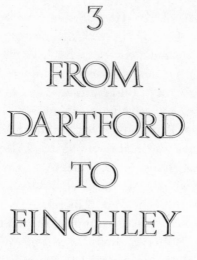

3

FROM
DARTFORD
TO
FINCHLEY

Any Conservative with political ambitions must attend the Party Conference as soon as possible, for that is where one may meet not only the leaders and the grandees, but, no less important, the Chairmen of the Constituency Associations, many of whom are on the look out for rising talent. The 1948 Conference at Llandudno proved no exception in this respect for Margaret Roberts, who went there representing the Oxford Graduates' Association, for there she met John Miller, Chairman of the Conservative Association at Dartford in Kent, and he suggested that she should put her name forward for that constituency. Apparently she took some persuading and wondered whether at 23 she was too young, but it was quickly pointed out that William Pitt had been Prime Minister at 24. So her name duly went forward. Up to then there had been twenty-six names on the list, all men with ages ranging from 28 to 55, but, when the Committee had seen and heard Miss Roberts, they unhesitatingly chose her. So, in March 1949 she was officially adopted and became, if not the youngest Conservative candidate, certainly the youngest woman standing for the Conservatives at the time. At the adoption meeting at Electricity House, she attacked the Labour Government's economic policies, especially bulk buying, insisted that taxes must come down to give the British working man some incentive, and stressed that Imperial Preference was the cornerstone of Conservatism. Her father, Alderman Roberts, who spoke, said that his family was Liberal, but that the Conservative Party now stood for much the same thing as the Liberal Party did in his young days. He was no doubt thinking of the free economy theme rather than Margaret's policy 'cornerstone' of Imperial Preference. Still, when Winston Churchill, an old Liberal, was leader of the Conservatives and seemed to find no difficulty in reconciling the two, the Roberts family was following the best of examples. When the time came to vote on her adoption there was only one dissentient out of the 400 crowded in the hall. A collection was taken amounting to £37 13s as a contribution to election expenses and this was promptly doubled by an anonymous supporter.

Practical as ever, she soon arranged a new job in London, this time as a food research chemist with J. Lyons and Company, which enabled her to live in the constituency. Even so, her day was long. She left home before 7.00 a.m. for work and returned at 7.00 p.m. to start on her political work, doing her rounds of branch, ward and women's meetings. One notable occasion was the visit of Mr Anthony Eden on 6 August for a mass open-air meeting where Margaret Roberts moved the vote of thanks. Her speech followed the usual official Conservative line at the time, attacking the Labour Government for its regime of austerity and controls, for its extravagance with the taxpayers' money, with a special anathema pronounced against Dr Dalton for squandering the American loan, and an onslaught on nationalisation, though the emphasis of her attack was interesting as it was a theme she was to return to persistently in the future. 'You cannot have the dream of building up your own fortune by your own hopes, your own hands, and your own British guts'; that was what was wrong with nationalisation. In another speech she put the point less colloquially, explaining that, in addition to the four freedoms of the Atlantic Charter, in which Conservatives believed, she would like to add a fifth, 'the freedom to use one's talents as one wished and to develop one's own ideas'.

She spoke in September at the Ladies' Luncheon Club in Ted Heath's neighbouring constituency of Bexley, appropriately enough on women's rights. 'Don't be scared of the high-flown language of economists and Cabinet Ministers,' she said refreshingly, 'but think of politics at our own household level. After all, women live in contact with food supplies, housing shortages and the ever-decreasing opportunities for children, and we must therefore face up to the position, remembering that as more power is taken away from the people, so there is less responsibility for us to assume.' Her speech was generally considered by her hearers to be 'the best ever heard from a woman' and she was thanked by the oldest member of the Falconwood Ward Women's Section, 85-year-old Mrs Arnott.

The young and pretty Conservative candidate was certainly successful at pulling in the crowds at this time. Not long before the 1950 election the *Daily Graphic* had a story about Miss Margaret Roberts, whom 400 came to hear on the same evening that Mr Dodds, the Labour Member for Dartford had an attendance of only 50. Her relationship with Mr Dodds was very amiable, however. In December 1949 they met for a public debate at Dartford Grammar School with Mr J. W. Pontin, a Conservative, in the chair (though everybody agreed that he conducted the proceedings impartially) and the Union Hall was packed to capacity with many people unable to get in. After the usual exchanges and questions each summed up briefly. Miss Roberts concluded with the hope that the people would soon elect a government which would enable the pound to look the dollar 'in the face and not in the bootlaces'. Mr Dodds tried the elder statesman ploy, saying that if there were any more of these debates Miss Roberts would want to join the Labour Party and he hoped that he would have the pleasure of enrolling her. This was not, as a matter of fact, their first meeting, because they had earlier been the guests of honour at a civic ball at Crayford Town Hall, where Mr Dodds and Miss Roberts, according to the *Evening News*, were to be found gliding across the dance floor in perfect harmony.

Aided by such civilities, it was a good-tempered contest. When the formal campaign began on 10 February Miss Roberts spoke eloquently of the electoral choice as the vital one between two ways of life and coined a slogan 'Vote right to keep what's left', which could, perhaps more pointedly, be used again now, a quarter-century further on.

Housing figured rather prominently in Miss Roberts's campaign. At Belvedere one questioner said he was dis-illusioned by Socialist promises on this subject, at which there was uproar from the 'Opposition' in the hall. Miss Roberts was heard to retort above the din, 'You people who have got a house should listen to someone who hasn't.' As for the Conservatives, their policy was to let the builder build as fast as he could and so ease pressure on the housing lists. She had some words for the Liberals too, who had just put up a candidate at the very last minute. If the Liberals really believed, as they professed, in the danger to personal liberty, then they should vote Conservative, she said, with all the confidence of a girl from a Liberal home.

The election result, when it came out, was as follows:

Dodds, N. (Co-op. and Lab.)	38,128
Roberts, M. (Cons.)	24,490
Giles, A.H. (Lib.)	5,011
Co-op. and Lab. majority	13,638

Any candidate who is worth his or her salt thinks he/she is going to win, even in one of the other side's strongholds, and with its 19,000 Labour majority a Labour stronghold is exactly what Dartford qualified as. Even so, Miss Roberts could look

Margaret and Muriel, 1929

Mayor *en famille*, 1945

The girl most likely . . . (back row, far left), 1941

Debut at Dartford, 1951

'. . . but we must build surely', 1951

Wedding Day, 1951

Twin-set, 1953

Home truths, 1961

On skis, 1955

First day, 1959

New girl, old friends – Charles Hill, Sir Waldron Smithers,
Patricia Hornsby-Smith, 1959

Junior Minister, 1961

with some satisfaction on a reduction of the Labour majority by a third and a rise of 50 per cent in the Conservative vote. In any case, that was the view of the Dartford Conservatives, who quickly readopted her and, at the same time, presented her with a marcasite brooch to show how highly they thought of her work in the last campaign. Nothing could, however, disturb the genial view which her opponent, Mr Dodds, took of her, and following the election he stood her a lunch at the House of Commons. At the readoption meeting she spoke of 'Operation Doorstep', a mass-canvass plan to swing the vote. Nationally the Conservatives, despite a huge swing to them, just failed to win a majority in the House of Commons, but Labour's victory was so narrow that it could only be a matter of time and a few by-elections before another General Election was called.

In May she was telling the annual meeting of the Chevening Branch of the Sevenoaks Association about the need for a Government which was pro-British, that children should be taught loyalty to their country, and, anticipating another election soon, she exhorted them to be prepared and keep their noses to the grindstone. So the year sped by with more hard work to do but enlivened by some pleasant little functions like the dinner and dance of the Barnehurst North Branch at the Bull Hotel, Dartford in February 1951, where the members presented her with a powder compact. She talked of the serious straits that the country was in, but took comfort from the existence of first rate Conservative leaders ready to take over. Above all there was Mr Churchill offering a splendid example at the age of 76. Mr Clement Attlee (the Labour Prime Minister) had referred to Mr Churchill as a Prima Donna. Prima Donnas were important people, she said, and when the time came Mr Churchill would strike up with the refrain 'Oh my darling Clem resign'. He would look to them to join in the chorus and they must keep in training. Not quite Groucho Marx standard perhaps, but if the picture in the *Erith Observer* is anything to go by, they all enjoyed it.

[21]

In April she was away again on the housing tack, full of confidence and brimming with statistics, to prove to the Erith Tenants' Association that Labour, under whom only 200,000 houses were being built every year, had betrayed the people, whereas the Conservatives would certainly build 300,000 houses by having the right materials in the right place at the right time. The tide was now running heavily against the Labour Government, and the election duly came in October, just in time to put a stop to the Tory Conference at Scarborough. So the formality of adoption was gone through again. Three hundred and fifty members of the Dartford Conservative Association went to Church Hall, Lowfield Street to adopt Miss Margaret Roberts for the second time around. As nobody wanted to miss Mr Churchill's speech that evening, a radio was installed on the platform (television was still in its infancy). The business of the meeting was concluded at 9.12 p.m. and the radio was switched on. Mr Churchill's speech produced round upon round of applause, and they concluded in very high spirits by singing 'Land of Hope and Glory'.

Miss Roberts's birthday fell during the election and, to her delight and surprise, she received bouquets of flowers at her campaign headquarters and a hat box and weekend case from the women of the Division.

Her meetings were packed and the good natured spirit of the contest continued. Indeed, Miss Roberts felt constrained to comment at one point that Dartford was getting the reputation for having the cleanest election in the country. Her topics were peace (the Socialists were trying to smear Churchill as a warmonger), housing, pensions, family allowances (which, as she was fond of saying, were no invention of the Socialists, but were thought up by a woman Independant—Eleanor Rathbone—who then persuaded the Parties to follow her), the crucial importance of Imperial Preference, the nationalisation by Persia's Mr Mossadeq of Anglo Iranian Oil, nationalisation versus free enterprise, and the Trade Unions. On these last she made the sensible observation that as they were getting ever more pink it was the job of the Conservative Trade Union movement to neutralise them. In fact that is just what the Conservative Trade Union movement was forbidden to do by the Central Office chiefs. Had the policy advocated by their youngest woman candidate been adopted instead, the domination of the Trade Union, movement by extremists, and many of the troubles arising from an irresponsible Trade Union movement, might have been nipped in the bud, instead of bursting out all over.

The day of the ballot duly arrived. The Dartford result was an improvement, the Socialist majority falling to 12,334, though on a higher total vote. In the country there was a great Conservative victory and Mr Churchill came to power. On the day of the 1951 General Election Margaret Roberts got engaged. It was a bit of a surprise, because not long before she had been saying that she was too busy with politics to marry. Her fiancé was Denis Thatcher, managing director of a family paint firm. He was an old Mill Hillian, had been a staff officer serving in Southern France and Italy during the war, when he had collected an MBE and a mention in dispatches. He was ten years older, he was established, he was devoted. They were married on 13 December at the Wesleyan Chapel in City Road, London. After two years Mrs Thatcher bore twins—a girl, Carol, and a boy, Mark.

In the meantime she had taken to the law, which had long been her ambition. Curiously enough she passed her Bar finals at exactly the same time as, and appeared on the pass list sandwiched between, Mr Jeremy Thorpe, now Leader of the Liberal Party, and Mr Dick Taverne, who was to achieve fame as the man who left the Labour Party over the Common Market and then fought and won back his old seat at Lincoln, representing his own new party, the Democratic Socialists.

Mrs Thatcher was a pupil in tax chambers, which numbered among its partners Mr Anthony Barber (now Lord Barber), later to be Chancellor of the Exchequer in the 1970-4 Heath Government. He said recently that, despite women's problems at the Bar in fields which were considered to be a male preserve, like taxation (as opposed to, say, divorce, which is recognised to be a woman's subject), he was sure she would have done very well. As he also observed, he himself found at the Treasury that the background of the tax Bar made the intricacies of fiscal legislation much easier to grasp and this must obviously have been a help when Mrs Thatcher became Opposition Spokesman on Treasury matters.

At the time of the 1955 election the twins were too young to be left during the campaign. The next election, however, was a different matter.

Most Members of Parliament have to work their passage by standing in a hopeless or marginal seat or two before being considered fit for the safe ones. By standing twice and doing so well at Dartford Mrs Thatcher had now served her apprenticeship and was in the top flight of potential candidates. Her legal qualifications were not wasted either, for then even more than now, constituency committees still regarded lawyers, especially barristers, with a certain irrational awe. Moreover, the habit of advocacy gives the candidate with a legal background the confidence in speaking which is invariably the key to success, especially if, as often happens, the selection committee is far from sure of what it is trying to find. So when Sir John Crowder announced that he was retiring from his seat in Finchley where he had been returned at the previous election with a majority of over 12,000, Mrs Thatcher joined the applicants' eager rush. There was no holding her this time. Out of nearly 100 aspirants she was the Finchley Conservatives' choice. She had finally made it: Westminster was the next stop.

4

CLASS OF '59

When Parliament reassembled on 20 October, there was, as always, a good deal of interest in the new members in the press and none was more photographed than the new member for Finchley. The *Daily Telegraph* showed pictures of some of the new faces arriving at the Palace of Westminster, including Jeremy Thorpe, Judith Hart, Geoffrey Johnson Smith, Christopher Chataway, and Margaret Thatcher wearing a snappy new cocktail hat to go with her elegant dark dress, brooch, and pearls. Like over 300 others she put her name in for a Private Member's Bill and to her delight she came second. An *Evening News* reporter was the first to tell her about her success in the draw when she was just about to leave for home and asked what subject she would raise for introducing her first measure. She said, 'I am keeping that under my hat for the moment.' After some quick thinking she chose the 'Public Bodies (Admission of the Press to Meetings) Bill to provide for the admission of representatives of the press to the meetings of certain bodies exercising public functions'. In essence the Bill was intended to make effective the right of the press to attend the meetings of Local Councils and their Sub-Committees. An

Act of 1908 was supposed to confer this right, but it had been evaded in various ways and by mischance the legislative defect had never been repaired, though there was an undertaking to put things right in the 1959 Conservative Manifesto. What gave it topical interest was the fact that earlier in the year there had been a printing strike and the newspapers concerned had been declared 'black'. Some Labour controlled local Councils then decided to support the blacking by refusing to allow the journalists who were defying the ban to attend their meetings. Yet, despite this sectional interest of some unions, there were plenty of Labour members who strongly supported the wider public interest which the Bill sought to protect. Indeed, one of them in the subsequent debate went as far as to say that there were at least as many village Hitlers as village Hampdens. She had, as was more to be expected, the support of nine Conservative MPs, including Sir Lionel Heald, a former Attorney General. The Bill was published in late January 1960 and the Second Reading (i.e. the first actual debate) took place on Friday, 5 February. Mrs Thatcher turned up in a coat frock of bronze and black brocade, buttoned down the front, with a black velvet collar. Her speech introducing the Bill was also her maiden speech and one which, as the *Daily Telegraph*'s Peterborough column commented, was unlikely to be excelled by any of her contemporaries new to the 1959 Parliament. She aroused general admiration by her thirty-minute exposition, without a note, of what was a controversial and complex Bill. As her opponent, Mr Reynolds, generously said, it was a speech of front-bench quality. She achieved indeed the rare feat of making a parliamentary reputation on a Friday, when many of the members depart early for their constituencies. On this occasion, no doubt due to the interest aroused by both the subject and the proposer, the attendance of over 100 was unusually good. It included Mr Peter Thorneycroft from among the old hands and Mr Christopher Chataway from among the youngsters. The women from both sides of the

House turned up trumps too. All three women members of the Government, Miss Pat Hornsby-Smith, Miss Edith Pitt and Miss Mervyn Pike, sat on the front bench practically throughout, while from the Labour side Mrs Barbara Castle and Mrs Joyce Butler both not only attended but spoke warmly in her support. When the time came to decide, the Bill was given its Second Reading by 152 votes to 39. Members rushed to congratulate Mrs Thatcher on what was clearly a resounding success. Of course there was the Committee stage to come and some tricky amendments. There was also, according to a letter in the *Guardian*, the embarrassing fact that the Conservative Group controlling the Finchley Borough Council not only refused to pass a motion congratulating Mrs Thatcher on her Bill, but, through its leader Alderman Norman, stated emphatically that the press would never be permitted to attend the meetings of the Council's General Purposes Committee.

Still, it was a marvellous beginning, and all sorts of newspapers ran human interest stories. Mrs Thatcher's opinions on family life, food, how to cope with Christmas, the atom bomb (which she was for) were eagerly sought. She was invited to address a luncheon at the Savoy for the Greater London Fund for the Blind as one of six Women of the Year. The speakers were all asked to confess their secret dreams to the 550 other women present, and say who they would most like to be if they were not themselves. Mrs Thatcher said she wanted to be Anna Leonowens of *Anna and the King of Siam* because she had 'a sense of purpose and the perseverance to carry out this purpose. She went to Siam with a sense of purpose and, because of her, slavery was abolished there.' Mrs Thatcher must have been reading Anna Leonowens's highly romanticised self-flattering account (or something based on it) which was apparently most inaccurate both about the King of Siam, who was a most enlightened man, and about Anna's own achievements there. She was, however, a lot more positive and imaginative, not to mention modest, than two of the others,

[27]

the Marchioness of Reading and Miss Evelyn Laye, the actress, neither of whom could think of anyone they would rather be than themselves.

In May she opened the Junior Fashion Fair, and, practical as ever, called for less ugly schoolwear and better and more understandable sizing codes, and urged manufacturers to concentrate on producing washable clothes in every category instead of the kind which had to be cleaned.

Mrs Thatcher had explained in an article in the *Evening News* earlier in the year how it *was* possible to do two jobs, but it was necessary to be well organised. Yet, even on her, the strain could sometimes tell, and in November she had a fainting attack in the House, and had to go home to rest. Apparently it was just overtiredness and she was soon back in harness.

Some months later Mrs Thatcher was prominent among the group of Conservative MPs, a minority it is true, but large enough to be called 'the biggest revolt since 1951', over reinstating corporal punishment. She told the Commons Standing Committee on the Criminal Justice Bill that a new young type of criminal had emerged. 'He does not use violence for robbery, but violence for the sake of violence,' she said. 'He causes pain as a form of pleasure.' She was more concerned about protecting the public than rehabilitating the criminal. She therefore suggested that young thugs have the choice between jail and the birch. This robust attitude undoubtedly reflected grass-roots opinion in the Party and, just as certainly, was bound to attract the abuse of the social science establishment. In fact she was later on to modify her position on this issue on practical grounds. This is very much the story of our times, which have brought a change in emphasis away from a simple moralistic approach in deciding the desirability of legislation—some actions are wrong and should be punished—to causalist thinking—if we change the law in this way the effects on the welfare of all the people concerned will be beneficial/damaging. The difficulty still is that while the electors are 'moralists' and are still thinking in simple retributional terms about, for instance, capital punishment, divorce, abortion and drugs, in recent times most MPs have become 'causalists', calculating more and more in terms of how much suffering is increased or decreased by tolerance or prohibition (see Christie Davies, *Permissive Britain*, Pitman, 1975). Even so, Mrs Thatcher's last point retains much of its original force. In the calculus of pain, social reformers are, perhaps, so much concerned about the pain to the criminal because the criminal is the prime object of their study that they forget, or underestimate, the suffering of the victim. Besides, the urge to impose fierce statutory penalties often springs from exasperation with the feeble attitude of many magistrates when it comes to imposing penalties for violence, and the desire to give them no option but to be severe.

At this time Mrs Thatcher was perhaps less embarrassed by those who dubbed her 'reactionary' than by an effusive article by Mr Godfrey Winn which compared her with the Queen—'the same flawless complexion'—at the mention of which she still winces, though when read now it looks harmless enough and was indeed rather well written. Mr Winn finished up by asking her the question, 'What is your own final ambition?' To which she replied, 'I'd like to go on being 35 for a long time.'

At this time she was among other things engaged, along with about twenty other MPs, including Messrs Gerald Nabarro, Neil Marten and Ted Leather, in going around the country selling the export drive to management and workers. This was in response to a request by Mr Reginald Maudling, then President of the Board of Trade, and the group was christened 'Maudling's Crusaders' by the *Daily Mail*. All this helped to get Mrs Thatcher known. Even more helpful was her appearance for the first time on a Party Political Broadcast on television, on which she talked about her Bill to let the press into council meetings, which had now gone through and was due to come into force in June.

Her interests ranged widely. In the same month as her broadcast she appeared with a Labour MP, Mrs Eirene White, at a Press Conference at the House of Commons, introducing the report of a survey on the needs of pre-school children living in flats of eight to twenty-five storeys. It was concerned with the sorts of practical matters which appealed to her, like providing the children with playgrounds and safer balconies. This was many years before the Ronan Point disaster and the studies, especially in America, which showed that high-rise flats are not only physically dangerous but tend to promote vandalism and social disintegration; so this report could properly be called 'forward looking'.

All this activity did bring its reward. In October 1961 the Prime Minister, Harold MacMillan, made some Cabinet changes. Among the new appointments was Mrs Thatcher, who took over as Joint Parliamentary Secretary to the Ministry of Pensions and National Insurance in succession to Dame Patricia Hornsby-Smith. It brought her a salary of £2,500 in addition to her MP's stipend of £750. Her husband Denis was away in Africa on an export tour, so she sent him an airmail letter to say she had joined the Government.

A reporter from the *Evening News* came to spend a day with the new Minister and found it all rather breathless. It was a case of up at 7.30, breakfast (one apple), read the newspapers, a hectic drive to drop the twins, now aged 8, at school (this was a regular thing, 'I always make sure I have time for the children'), coffee, sign letters, open the mail, last-minute instructions to Nanny, drive to the House of Commons to pick up mail, cash a cheque and then board the train to Lincolnshire to go and give prizes at a school speech day. The following day she was off on an export promotion speech in Nottingham. If these two days were typical, this particular week was not, because there was the Annual Tory Conference to attend and at this an appearance was obligatory, not to say advisable. She turned up on the Friday in a royal blue car, wearing a royal blue dress and a royal blue hat. From this session she had to rush back to pick up the twins and then spend the weekend answering all the letters of congratulation she had received.

When Mrs Thatcher finally came to make her debut in the Commons in a major debate as Minister, which mercifully was not until March, she had obviously mastered her brief with her usual efficiency. She was answering a Labour motion of censure, deploring the Government's failure to raise pensions. At the end of her speech, as the Liverpool *Daily Post* commented, 'She left MPs stunned with statistics', giving figures to show the value of the pension in 1946, 1951, 1959 and 1962, the cost of living in smoking and non-smoking households, the total sums spent on pensions, the total amount raised in surtax, the levels of pensions in Sweden, Denmark, West Germany, 'for forty-four minutes she hardly stopped to draw a breath'. Indeed, just how stunned they were was shown by the fact that the Speaker had to call twice for the next debate before any member rose to his feet. Or to *her* feet, for there were still few women in the House and Socialist Mrs Jean Mann shortly afterwards sought to sum up female power prospects in a book *Women in Parliament*. In this, on the basis of her fifteen years' experience as an MP, she concluded that there was little likelihood of a woman taking any of the top ministerial jobs such as Chancellor of the Exchequer, or Foreign Minister. We always have to take the 'best man we've got' for the job. She added a few comments on her female colleagues in the House. Of Mrs Thatcher she had this spry observation to make, which seemed to be flatteringly contradictory to her main thesis; 'She does not believe in taking two bites at a cherry. She takes two at one bite. She has twins, for instance, and is a qualified chemist and barrister. She made her maiden speech and a private member's Bill in one go, and it was a speech of front bench quality. At this pace Margaret Thatcher is capable of quads and the Foreign Office.'

Yet if skies looked blue for Mrs Thatcher personally, they

were looking grey for Mr Macmillan's administration. The confidence of the Wondermac and the 'you never had it so good' era had foundered on the rock of economic adversity. Mr Selwyn Lloyd at the Exchequer lacked the magic touch. In his attempt to deal with the worsening balance of payments crisis he had resorted to budgetary restraint, credit squeeze and a pay pause. In the spring of 1962 there were three bad by-elections crowned by Orpington, formerly a safe suburban Tory seat, but where the Conservatives lost roughly 10,000 votes and the seat fell to the Liberals. In early July the Conservative Central Office reported to Mr Macmillan that the next by-election in North East Leicester would bring a new setback, and Messrs R. A. Butler (Home Secretary) and Iain Macleod (Party Chairman) called on him to press for Government changes. Mr Macmillan decided that the time had come to act drastically and he fired Mr Selwyn Lloyd from the Treasury, putting Mr Reginald Maudling in his place. There was a large number of other changes with 'RAB' becoming Deputy Prime Minister and First Secretary of State and, more to the point as far as Mrs Thatcher was concerned, with her boss at the Ministry of Pensions, John Boyd-Carpenter, being promoted to be Chief Secretary of the Treasury.

There was one woman victim of the reshuffle, Miss Edith Pitt, who at Question Time on 16 July already knew that she had been axed, though the House did not. If her voice sounded dejected, she managed to end her career as Junior Minister at the Ministry of Health with the optimistic phrase 'the number of nurses in the Health Service continues to rise'. Mrs Thatcher was the first Minister to arrive and the first to speak. Amid the gloom and uncertainty on the Government benches she alone radiated confidence, cheerfulness and charm. There were nineteen questions to do with the Ministry of Pensions and National Insurance and she answered them all. Mr Percy Browne, asking the first question, prefaced his supplementary with the words: 'In view of the temporary nature of Ministerial

[32]

appointments, will she be sure to leave a note calling his or her attention to . . . .' Mrs Thatcher replied that she would tell her next Rt Hon. Friend—when she had one!

Mr Macmillan managed to rally his Party well enough in the ensuing debate, which was on the Labour motion of no confidence, and the new blood—people like Mr Enoch Powell, Sir Keith Joseph and Sir Edward Boyle—gave some needed stimulus to the administration, at least on the social service side. Unfortunately, though, his ruthlessness left a lasting scar. In the Party at large the feeling was that Mr Selwyn Lloyd's treatment was, in the words of Mr Gerald Nabarro, 'shabby and disreputable', and the fund of loyalty which had been the Tories' secret weapon was now almost exhausted. Besides, while Mr Selwyn Lloyd had for the most part been the loyal executive of his leader's economic policies he had lately been converted to the principles of orthodox finance. On the morning after his dismissal there appeared a letter from Mr Nigel Birch, one of the three ministers who had resigned from Mr Macmillan's previous administration over its failure to balance the books (the other two resigners, Messrs Peter Thorneycroft and Enoch Powell, had come back in the reshuffle). The letter ran:

Sir,
For the second time the Prime Minister has got rid of a Chancellor of the Exchequer who tried to get expenditure under control.
Once is more than enough.
Yours truly, Nigel Birch.

With the passing of the years we can now see that the fatal flaw in the second Macmillan administration, and not of the Macmillan administration alone, was the failure to control that excess of Government spending which is the fuel of inflation. It is easy and perhaps basically right to argue that, having gone wrong on this, nothing else would go right. Even so, in order to enjoy success Governments not only need the right policies, they need luck into the bargain, and what gradually became apparent was that Mr Macmillan's supplies of the latter commodity had dried up.

At first, though, the clouds seemed to be clearing. At the Conservative Conference in October Mr Macmillan decided to seek an out-and-out endorsement for his policy of entering the European Community. In this endeavour he was helped by the anti-European outburst of Mr Gaitskell, the Labour leader, at Labour's Conference the week before (when he said that entry would conflict with 1,000 years of British history); for nothing recommends a policy more persuasively to the Tory rank and file than Socialist opposition to it. Mr Macmillan, in order to ensure that the faithful knew where their duty lay, issued his own pro-European pamphlet to the delegates, and even Mr R.A. Butler, who was never considered a particularly zealous European, popped up with a happy rejoinder to the Gaitskell line: 'For them a thousand years of history books. For us the future.' The result was not in doubt. The conference voted overwhelmingly for joining the European Community.

This vote was to prove Mr Macmillan's last triumph. The following month the public opinion polls swung sharply against him, and the Conservatives proceeded to lose five by-elections. Meanwhile Mrs Thatcher was happily at work in her Ministry, but not making any headlines. There was a pleasant picture of her that December shooting down the ski-run at Battersea Park, a 60-ft-long affair made of brushed nylon. In politics generally it was a strange time, marked by a widespread feeling of disillusionment which burgeoned in a sudden upsurge of satire. For this was the era of the stage review *Beyond the Fringe*, of the first issue of the magazine *Private Eye* and the beginning of the BBC's *That Was The Week That Was*. All these combined in a sort of orgy of destruction to send up the 'establishment' and all its works, including that supreme establishment figure Mr Macmillan. No time, therefore, could have been more

[34]

unfortunate for the emergence of a really ripe public scandal. Yet that is precisely what did emerge in June in the form of the Profumo Affair. The public opinion polls after the Profumo confession gave Labour their biggest lead for twenty-five years. Mrs Thatcher must have been wondering what was coming next, and in July she made a speech to women unionists at a luncheon in Edinburgh which had perhaps even more application to a later date. 'No one person, however great, could win an election for a political Party. Equally, no one disaster affecting one person could lose an election for a great Party.' She went on to say that, in the past, the Conservatives had made too much of the cult of personality: 'We have made too much of one or two people, and we think that they can win or lose elections for us. Don't be depressed if one particular person transgresses. It doesn't lose an election unless the Party loses faith in itself.'

She had constituency worries at this time, which might sound strange because Finchley was considered a pretty solid Conservative seat. Yet in the local elections in May 1963 the Liberals polled 18,000 votes—5,000 more than the Conservatives. Why? If one asked Mrs Thatcher, or so Anthony Howard said in an article in the *New Statesman*, she would say mysteriously, 'It's the golf club you know. That's where it all started, and where the whole thing has come from.' Apparently it did all go back to discrimination against Jews by the golf club, which refused membership to a number of applicants who put 'Jewish' in the column on the form marked 'religion'. This was played up by the Liberals with some success as there were around 14,000 Jewish electors in the division. Could this be another Orpington, a constituency with which Mrs Thatcher was closely acquainted because her house where she spent the weekends was located there? The Liberals adopted a good candidate of whom more was to be heard in the future—his name was John Pardoe.

Mrs Thatcher played it cool, kept on doing her rounds in the constituency, mending her fences and explaining Government policy, especially to those interest groups directly affected. For instance, in May 1964 she met the Finchley Chamber of Commerce and went into various aspects of Ted Heath's controversial (but on balance immensely valuable) Bill for the abolition of Resale Price Maintenance. She explained that many of the objections of traders were being ironed out by amendments. There were in fact five grounds of exemption of price maintenance under the Act. She had to expound the Private Member's Bill which required that trading stamps should have their value printed on them, that stamps should be redeemable for cash and that the catalogue issued by the stamp firms should state the cash value of the full stamp book. She was enthusiastically in favour of these proposals on characteristic grounds: 'I am all for people knowing what they are getting, and being able to ascertain the value they are getting in return for the money they pass over.'

1963 was altogether a disastrous year for the Tory Government. It began badly enough with President De Gaulle's vote on British entry; in June came the Profumo Affair; finally on the eve of the Conservative Party Conference in October Mr Macmillan fell ill and a successor had to be found. It could not fail to be the most exciting Conservative Conference since the war. Out of the chaos emerged—for those were the days of emergence not election—Lord Home, or rather (since the legislation brought in to enable Mr Anthony Wedgwood Benn, to convert himself from Lord Stansgate back into a commoner was now to hand) Sir Alec Douglas-Home. Sir Alec fought the subsequent General Election on the issue of national security, the subject he best knew; Mr Harold Wilson, Labour's leader, fought it on an imaginative-sounding plan, which only time would show was pure rhetoric, to forge a new Britain in the white heat of the technological revolution. Sir Alec in fact did amazingly well in only just losing—considering that, as all the research shows, the British people are rarely moved when it

comes to voting by anything but bread-and-butter issues.
Labour mounted a most successful attack on the Tories'
'Twelve Wasted Years'. Mrs Thatcher, by way of riposte, talked
to her constituents of 'Twelve years of unparalleled
achievement'. A Swiss television camera team descended on her
adoption meeting, and it was a good choice as it typified the
better sort of Conservative constituency gathering. Mrs
Thatcher, her husband Denis at her side, addressed a packed
hall. She mainly talked about economic affairs, especially
about Britain's crying need for more exports (to which, of
course, as one of Reggie Maudling's 'Crusaders', she had given
much study). Socialist planning would not provide them; they
could only come from the private enterprise sector. It was
conventional and sound and on the theme of the socialist threat
to prosperity which Sir Alec would have done better to put in
the forefront of his appeal to the Nation. At the end of the
meeting the Chairman, Councillor U. H. Usher, proposed Mrs
Thatcher as their candidate in the forthcoming election: 'We
need someone whom we can look up to, who is modern, whom
we can respect.' When he asked for a seconder the meeting rose
to its feet as one man. In the event her majority was nearly
halved and the main challenge had indeed come from the
Liberals, but the margin was still comfortable at 8,802. She was
going back to Westminster all right, but this time to sit on the
Opposition benches.

5

OPPOSITION FRONT BENCH

Probably the chief reason for the Conservative loss of the election of 1964 was that the public grew tired of them, and this *ennui* among the electors was mainly due to the Conservatives' loss of confidence in themselves. The Profumo Affair, De Gaulle's vote on our entry into the Common Market, the leadership muddle, the failure to get on top of the economic problem, which was reflected in a (to contemporary eyes) perilous rate of inflation and yawning deficit on the balance of payments; all contributed to a demoralisation of the Conservatives which sapped their will to win. Mr Harold Wilson, on the other hand, was at his most convincing and, on economic matters, more expert (though not any wiser) than Sir Alec, who had, after all, spent nearly all his political life dealing with Foreign Affairs. Besides, when it came to promising what they would do with taxpayers' money the Socialists, who did not think the taxpayer had any right to the money in the first place, could always outbid the Conservatives, who were still weighed down by scruples and some lingering impulse to practise the principles of sound finance. Unfortunately the comings and goings on economic policy, with the Selwyn Lloyd squeeze being swiftly succeeded by the Reginald Maudling expansion, and the impression given by Mr Wilson, with his international league table comparisons, that Britain had been performing rather badly, damaged the Conservative image and made people that much more ready to believe in the plausible-sounding Labour alternative.

Mr Wilson descended on Downing Street with a great flurry of activity and talk—like a poor man's President Kennedy—of 100 days of dynamic action. Meanwhile Sir Alec, recognising that with a Labour majority of only five there must be another election soon, appointed Mr Edward Heath to chair the policy groups who were to provide the policies on which the next election was to be fought. Mrs Thatcher, naturally enough, became Shadow Spokesman on Pensions, where she was matched against another formidable lady, Miss Peggie Herbison, and by November they were busy arguing the toss over Labour's National Insurance Bill. This aimed at putting up social benefits and was not basically very controversial because the Conservatives had also intended to put them up had they remained in power; still, it was a chance for the girls to show their form. Miss Herbison put up a fine vigorous performance, explaining the measure at some length and congratulating the pensioners on escaping from a generation of. Tory rule. Mrs Thatcher, in her turn, congratulated Miss Herbison on 'a fighting speech' and added, 'I think she was fighting her own side.'

In May Mrs Thatcher was leading twenty Conservative MPs in tabling a motion which urged the strongest Government protest to Russia over the arrest of the British lecturer Mr Gerald Brooke in Moscow. Mr Brooke, a lecturer in Russian at the Holborn College of Law, Languages and Commerce, who had gone to the Soviet Union leading a party of tourists, was arrested by KGB men when he and his wife, Barbara, were visiting a Russian family's apartment. After arrest, he was detained, without seeing his wife or anyone from his own country, for eight days. Mrs Thatcher, whose constituent Mr Brooke was, urged the Government to suspend cultural exchanges with all the countries which did not observe proper consular practice. This was a shrewd move, because the Russians value cultural exchanges both for their propaganda effect in other countries and because they confer a degree of moral legitimacy on their despotic and bloodstained regime. It did not have immediate effect (partly because of Mr Wilson's known enthusiasm for links with the USSR) but it seems likely to have contributed usefully to Mr Brooke's eventual release. In the same month Mrs Thatcher spoke in the Albert Hall to 5,000 members of the National Union of Townswomen's Guilds on 'Woman—no longer a satellite'—as well she might. She produced a memorable remark which was eagerly seized on by the press: 'In politics, if you want anything said, ask a man: if you want anything done, ask a woman.' A week later she was in Stratford-on-Avon prophesying, rather hopefully, that the Labour Government would soon run out of money. In July the Conservative Parliamentary Party had the new experience of electing a Leader, and the result was a decisive victory for Mr Edward Heath, though strangely enough, if opinion polls meant anything, the public preferred Mr Maudling.

In October Mrs Thatcher was appointed Opposition Spokesman on Housing and Land, and in this capacity replied at the Conservative Conference to a motion on reforming the rating system. She reviewed very thoroughly means of relieving the injustice and hardship which the rate burden brought, but thought that the institution of a local income tax would be of little avail because there would have to be two methods of assessment and collection. It was the sort of point that naturally appealed to one who had practised at the tax Bar.

On returning to Parliament in November she was engaged,

along with Mr John Boyd-Carpenter, in attacking Labour's highly bureaucratic Land Commission scheme. She foresaw a conflict coming between the proposed Land Commission and other local planning authorities. There were also some shocking proposals for compulsory purchase of land, and a proposed levy threatened to put a severe brake on modernisation and expansion.

Mrs Thatcher was still the watchdog on pensions, and in December she was campaigning on behalf of the 3,500 Britons in Rhodesia whom the Wilson Government, in a moment of extreme pettiness, had deprived of their pensions, though by contrast, as she was quick to point out, the Government had done nothing to stop the transfer to Moscow of the private income of the traitor Guy Burgess.

The election was now imminent, and the Party dog-fight was becoming more fierce. The object of Conservative attacks, naturally, was Mr Wilson, and Mrs Thatcher joined in the fun with a speech to the Scottish Women Conservatives in Glasgow in February, saying that Mr Wilson was 'a very good talker, but he is not a doer'. This foreshadowed the Conservative election slogan 'Action not words' which, however, proved to have little enough appeal, and perhaps rightly. For words are part of the deeds, often the most important deeds, of the politician, and Mr Wilson was undoubtedly a wordsmith, even if the results of his craftsmanship rarely succeeded in stirring any of the nobler impulses of his hearers. The Heath-Wilson contest was indeed a strange one. On the one hand there was Mr Heath, with his emphasis on action really implying that politics is essentially administration, and on the other Mr Wilson, basically believing, as Mr Cecil King was later to remark, that politics is about winning debates in the House of Commons. For Mr Heath the real world was in the corridors of Whitehall: for Mr Wilson it was within the halls of the Palace of Westminster.

And so into the election of March 1966. The Conservatives

under Mr Heath had done their policy group homework and had a clutch of new policies, though already exhibiting the defect of being one-off affairs somewhat artificially stitched together in one document, and uneasily harbouring the two rival philosophies of free enterprise capitalism on the one hand and state corporatism on the other. The manifesto gave an easy sloganised summary of the 'action' to which the Party was committing itself:

> Get the economy straight, and check rising prices, and restore expansion.
> Reform the Trade Unions.
> Remodel the Welfare State.
> Get the Nation properly housed.
> Restore respect in Britain and lead her into Europe.

The trouble with such check lists of actions to be taken is that they give an illusory impression that the mere statement of objectives on the same sheet of paper means that they can all be achieved together. Yet, in the minds of some economists, there were mounting doubts. Professor Paish, for instance, wondered about how far it was possible to pursue both growth and stable prices at the same time. It might, he thought, and as we have subsequently discovered, be necessary to choose between the two. Again the bland promise 'to make a prices and incomes policy effective' was included alongside the undertaking to introduce 'new policies for competition' without any sense of incongruity. The trouble with 'Action not words' was that all too often, as Nietzsche had long before said, 'Action is a substitute for thought'.

In the event, the British people were in more of a mood to give Labour a chance, with their usual instinct, however bizarre in its application, in favour of fair play. The Labour manifesto also made a great song and dance about the mess the Conservatives had left as a result in particular of the Maudling expansion policy, which coincided with a £750 million deficit in the balance of payments. Without going into all the ins and outs of the argument, there was one main difficulty with the Maudling policy of dashing for growth, even if we accept the simplistic idea on which it was based— that the prime need was to create a high level of demand in order to stimulate investment, which, in turn, would provide the seedcorn of future growth. That difficulty was that Britain's price level was already too high compared with those of her competitors. Thus, with a fixed exchange rate, and given the rigidity of the British industrial structure, expansion was bound to have as its first effect a sharp rise in the import bill. So there was some justice in Labour's indictment, even though Labour was in no position to complain. Had Labour been in charge, the dash for growth would have been even more precipitate—Mr Callaghan was talking about pushing the growth rate up to 6 per cent! The £750 million deficit somehow got rounded up to £800 million and the reiteration of this figure, more than anything else, wrecked the Conservative chances of coming back. Labour increased their overall majority to a comfortable 96. Mrs Thatcher fared better than her party. The challenge from the Liberals, mounted imaginatively enough by a new opponent, Mr Frank Davis, who gained some prominence as the organiser of a local pirate bus service, did not in the end amount to very much. When the votes were counted the Liberals were found to have slipped to third place. Mrs Thatcher's majority on a reduced poll rose by 600 votes and there was actually a swing of 2·35 per cent in her favour.

On her return to the House, Mrs Thatcher was appointed an Opposition Spokesman on Treasury and Economic Affairs; this was a great opportunity because three weeks later there was the Budget debate. Mrs Thatcher was in sparkling form. The comparative ineptitude of Mr John

Diamond, the Chief Secretary to the Treasury, on this occasion provided her with an easy target for her witticisms, and truly, as *The Times* commented, Diamond was a girl's best friend. He set the scene with a boring discourse about the effect of the Selective Employment Tax (SET) on the cost of living, which he said time and time again would raise it by at the most two-thirds of 1 per cent. Mrs Thatcher said let him wait and see what happened to the price of a meal in the House of Commons dining room. That would show him. She ridiculed the way the tax took 25*s* away from some and then repaid them 32*s* 6*d*. Why not pay them 7*s* 6*d* and have done with it? 'Oh that Gilbert and Sullivan should be living at this hour,' she cried. 'This is sheer cockeyed lunacy. The Chancellor needs a woman at the Treasury.' She attacked the complexity of the tax system and waved a bright yellow form which was supposed to explain the Capital Gains Tax, then quoted one passage which was quite contrary to the last Finance Act. 'Really,' she said, 'how can we get it right when those who draw up the form don't know what the Act means?'

She went on to say, to the accompaniment of some gasps, that she had read every Budget speech and every Finance Bill since 1946. In none of them, she asserted, had even the most grasping Chancellor failed to make at least a minor concession on the social side. None, that was, until Mr Callaghan. She then cited what Mr Diamond said on the subject of investment allowances. 'I didn't,' protested Mr Diamond. 'Oh, well,' said Mrs Thatcher, unstoppable by now, 'I am sure that is what he would have said if he had thought about it.'

Passionately she denounced Mr Diamond as no friend to women, particularly married women and widows who had to go out to work, because they were forced to employ someone to look after their children. Mr Diamond retorted, 'The honourable lady must know that this is a tax on employers.'

[44]

'Precisely,' came the reply, 'These women *are* employers. Clearly the Front Bench have not even thought of this. Perhaps now they will do something about it.' Mr Diamond sat down, not the first to be washed away in the flood of this particular female's logic.

The speech was a tonic for her own back-benchers and for the front-benchers too. Iain Macleod, writing in the *Daily Mail*, said, 'I have heard many excellent speeches from women Ministers and members from the front and back benches of the House of Commons, but cannot recall another in a major debate that was described as a triumph.'

At the Conference at Blackpool in October, Mrs Thatcher made another blistering attack on the Government's Selective Employment Tax and its freeze legislation. 'The Government has undermined legal rights and respect for the law. The legal system we have and the rule of law are far more responsible for our traditional liberties than any system of one man one vote. Any country or Government which wants to proceed towards tyranny starts to undermine legal rights and undermine the law.' All this was a step, she went on, not just towards Socialism, but towards Communism. She denounced Mr Wilson for deceiving the electorate in 1964: if he had said, 'In the next two years I am going to increase taxation by £1,200 million, I am going to introduce a taxation system that no one will be able to understand. I am going to fine an employer if he dares pay an employee more without my permission, and on top of that I am going to pay myself 50 per cent more than any other Prime Minister for doing it', 'he would have been totally and utterly rejected or he should have been.' It was another triumph. The 4,000 delegates gave her a standing ovation. Her denunciation of Communism, however, was itself denounced by Bernard Levin as a means of getting a 'cheap' cheer' and as a debasement of language and politics alike. Mr Wilson, he argued, was too feeble to be compared with the brutal people in charge on the other side of the Iron Curtain. Yet was it not the feeble socialist politicians of the Weimar Republic who undermined the rule of law and prepared the way for Hitler? For that matter, was it not the feeble Mensheviks who let the Bolsheviks take over in Russia? It was precisely this same point that Mr Levin made years later (*The Times*, 8 April 1975) in taking the Labour Government to task over their indemnity of the Clay Cross Councillors, when he quoted Mr Robert Bolt's Thomas More: 'And when every law in England is down, and the Devil turns round and grins at you, where will you hide then?' Large villainies usually have small beginnings. Mrs Thatcher was right to put the debate on that level. It was a pity that some of her colleagues did not see the issue as clearly as she.

Denunciation was becoming Mrs Thatcher's stock in trade. In January 1967 she was using the feature column of the *Daily Express* to make an onslaught on the Land Commission Act. She was in this matter, as so often, in sympathy with the grass roots. It was the defence of the owner-occupier, the person trying to save, to build up a home or a business, to put something aside for their children, of such people, so like herself in interest if not in ability, which aroused her passionate sympathy and concern.

In October 1967 Mrs Thatcher was made a member of the Shadow Cabinet where she in effect took the place, though not the post, of Miss Mervyn Pike, who had asked to go mainly for health reasons. Mrs Thatcher's new responsibility was Power, much of which is of course in the public sector, and so it was appropriate that she should answer the debate at the 1967 Conservative Party Conference at Brighton on a motion from the Darwen Conservatives calling for denationalisation. Mrs Thatcher joined in eloquent attacks on the inefficiency of nationalised industries. She said 'The lesson has been that when you nationalise an industry not only do you pay a higher price for its products, but you pay twice to meet the ever-increasing deficits and the capital investment.' The danger of more nationalisation was ever-present with a Labour Government because she said, 'Every time there is a revolt from the Labour back benches, they are thrown a tit-bit and that tit-bit is usually more nationalisation.' The Conference carried the denationalisation motion unanimously.

In Parliament Mrs Thatcher was being used outside the limited area of her specific Shadow responsibilities. In May she wound up for the Opposition on a motion of censure of the Government's policy on prices. As Andrew Alexander, in the *Daily Telegraph*, said, she 'gave a dashing performance, firing salvo after salvo of devastating statistics into the Labour benches like a cannon firing grapeshot into a crowd'. She decided to nail the £800 million deficit which Labour accused the Conservatives of bequeathing them when they quit office in 1964. She pointed out that the actual deficit was £776 million, but the deficit on current account was £402 million, which was £17 million less than the Conservatives inherited from the Labour Government seventeen years before. She pointed out that in ten of the thirteen so-called 'wasted years' the Conservatives achieved surpluses on current account, and when they lost office they left a better current account position than they had found. Since 1964 there had been a current account deficit every year, and 1967's, at £154 million, was the worst ever.

When she was attacking the rise in electricity prices Mr Mendelson angrily said that the rises were needed to meet the financial targets set by the Tories (Labour cheers). She retorted amid the uproar that, on the contrary, the rises were due to an excess of generating capacity. This had resulted, she said, from the electricity industry's accepting the targets of the National Plan; that put paid to Mr Mendelson. This was otherwise a poor, dreary debate on the Conservative side. Once again Mrs Thatcher had shown her extraordinary

[47]

capacity to rise to the occasion and to show that she was a very dangerous speaker for even the most experienced parliamentary paladin to tangle with. 'Why', asked the *Daily Telegraph's* Peterborough Column, referring to her exposure of the £800 million myth, despite the fact that the House of Commons Library was open to 240 Tory MPs, 'has it been left to Mrs Thatcher to do the homework?'

She stepped up the attack on the nationalised industries front too, hotly opposing the Government's Bill to permit a rise in the gas industry's borrowing powers of £1,200 million. In June she addressed a management conference on 'Women in Business' and cheerily suggested that the really talented among women would always make their own niche—except in the Stock Exchange. Part of the trouble was, however, that for too many girls 'O' Levels were the pinnacle of attainment. Only 3·2 per cent went to university, yet there were careers which could be mixed with marriage and children, like law and teaching. This may all sound a bit 'pie', but it was kindly meant, and it is only necessary to witness Mrs Thatcher in action before a female audience to realise not only how heartened they are to see her there on the platform, cool, confident and manifestly capable, but how obviously proud so many of them are that she at least has made it to the top, showing that where she has led other women may follow.

At the 1968 Conservative Party Conference Mrs Thatcher gave the annual lecture of the Conservative Political Centre (the political education wing of the Party). This lecture is normally the main event outside the programme of formal conference debates. She took as her subject 'What's wrong with Politics' and the main thing she found wrong was the growing power of the state over the individual. Government was becoming more remote and this could best be cured not by participation but by reducing the area of Government decision. Governments should not seek to control prices, but see that competition flourishes, not try to control every salary but regulate the money supply and manage demand. After the Conference Mrs Thatcher went with the Commonwealth Parliamentary Association on a visit with eight other MPs to the Bahamas, where they met Chief Cakobad from Fiji, believed to be the original maker of the remark, when shown the menu, 'Take this away and bring me the passenger list.' At one point he turned to Mrs Thatcher and said, 'See what we have in common. We're the only ones in skirts.'

On their return Mr Heath announced more changes in his Shadow Cabinet, and Mrs Thatcher became Shadow Spokesman on Transport. The way she was being shifted around certainly suggested that she was being groomed for higher things when the party came to power. Her series of jobs, first as Junior Minister of Pensions, followed by Shadow appointments covering Treasury and Economic Affairs, followed by Housing and Land and then Fuel and Power, gave her a range and versatility which no other Conservative woman MP had yet enjoyed. The sole regret amoung MPs was that Mrs Thatcher had not gone to Transport soon enough to cross swords with Mrs Barbara Castle. For, though different in style, they were both able and imperious, and mistresses of the sharp retort—and had keen respect for one another. Instead she was up against Mr Richard Marsh, whom she said she knew of old because he used to heckle her meetings, and, she conceded, he was 'quite nice looking'. Mrs Thatcher was soon at work in her new capacity, backing a motion by Captain Walter Elliot, MP for Carshalton, demanding that the Government do something about the delays, discomfort and general inefficiency of the commuter transport systems. In January she made a big attack on the Crossman pension scheme, which, she said, amounted to passing the buck to employers. The invitations to speak were now coming more frequently and from many different sorts of bodies. In February 1969 she gave the ninth Viscountess Samuel

Memorial Lecture to the Union of Jewish Women, an important engagement in any case, but vital for the member for Finchley! In the same month she talked to the annual dinner of the Barnsley Chamber of Commerce, and in London a week later she was holding forth to the Federation of Business and Professional Women's Clubs about the awful jargon in use on the subject of management. She suggested that most of it could be boiled down to simple questions like 'What are we trying to do?' and 'How do we propose to do it?' The week after that she was off to America for a month's lecturing and studying transport.

At the previous Party Conference she had met the editor of the *Daily Telegraph*, Mr Maurice Green, who was deeply impressed by her and persuaded her to do two articles for his newspaper which expounded her philosophy of politics. They were noteworthy because in them she made more explicit than ever before her commitment to the confessedly right-wing aim of reducing the public sector, and, rare indeed in Conservative politicians at that time, made some specific suggestions for some measures of denationalisation.

In May she replied to the motion at the Scottish Conservative Conference at Leith, demanding that social security payments for 'spongers' should be curbed. She said, characteristically, 'We must recognise certain groups of people who need help, but the rest of us must take responsibility for ourselves, and we must stop being such a subsidised-minded society.' She also replied to a motion on the cost of living, leaving delegates in no doubt of her view that inflation was the greatest scourge of society: 'It meant that the honest who saved up for old age many years ago had had a rotten deal.'

In mid-June Mrs Thatcher got involved in the row over the planning blight which had fallen upon a hundred houses in her constituency. A week later she was investigating in Committee allegations that some road haulage firms had been held to ransom by union demands, backed by threats of instant shutdown. One road haulage firm was supposed to have settled a dispute by handing a cheque to the unions' convalescent home, though this was a cover for the actual payment of £1,000 each to two shop stewards and £400 each for seven others.

In July at last came the good news that Mr Gerald Brooke, Mrs Thatcher's constituent who had got into trouble with the Soviet authorities, was to be released. This was a happy prelude to her own working trip to Russia (the work being to study transport) in the company of Mr Paul Channon MP and his wife. Finally, to round off the Party's year, Mrs Thatcher went to the Conservative Party Conference at Brighton, where she spoke in reply to a motion in favour of more equal rights for women, a policy which was supported by the leadership, and a programme for which was outlined in a pamphlet issued by the Conservative Political Centre called *Fair Shares for the Fair Sex.* She concluded her speech with a quotation from Sophocles: 'Once a woman is made equal to man she becomes his superior.' At this there were loud cheers which sounded, however, as if they were coming from the women delegates. It was after this conference that Mrs Thatcher was made the Conservative Shadow on Education and now a new chapter in her life began.

6

SHADOWING
SHORT

In October, 1969 Mrs Thatcher was made Shadow Minister of Education. This was only a year after her appointment as Shadow Minister of Transport. It was not part of a general reshuffle; she simply took the place of the previous incumbent. Mr Peter Walker took over Mrs Thatcher's responsibility for Transport, and Sir Keith Joseph, who had been tipped for Education, merely took charge of Technology and Power in addition to Trade. Nobody new was appointed to the Shadow Cabinet, of which Mrs Thatcher was already a member, and its number therefore fell to 16. As the Conservative Leader, Mr Heath, was not much given to changing his team, this move calls for some explanation. The change came soon after the 1969 Conservative Party Conference, where Sir Edward Boyle, Shadow Education Minister, was given a roasting by the delegates in the education debate. The particular bone of contention was his pusillanimous attitude towards the Government's proposal in Circular 10/65. This Whitehall missive, without parliamentary sanction, 'requested' local authorities to submit proposals forthwith for complete comprehensivisation—that is to say,

[52]

for the destruction of the grammar schools. Sir Edward's response had been to say that, while the Conservatives would not themselves have launched such a scheme, he would not recommend them to withdraw it when they came to power. At the actual Conference, he changed his tune somewhat and gave the undertaking that, if the Labour Government should be so foolish as to bring in a law compelling local authorities to introduce schemes of comprehensive education, then he would oppose it and, on return to power, repeal it. In his view at least the transition from nudging and ear stroking to actual legislation was all important, but it seemed more likely that he was being pretty effectively nudged himself by angry members of his own party. It is instructive to understand how their sympathy came to be lost.

First, quite apart from the area of policy concerned, Sir Edward was a progressive of the kind which is not infrequently bred among the English upper classes, and which some people consider to be dangerous. For, whatever he really thinks about it himself deep down, in his behaviour he certainly gave and gives a powerful impression of a man afflicted with a sense of guilt about his advantages in life. This at least would account for the fact that no one could surpass him in the solicitude with which he would address Labour members in the House, assuring them constantly of his sincerity, of his concern, of his warm-hearted understanding of points of view apparently opposed and his desire to be at one with them, in a cosy glow of consensus. And these protestations had their reward. Whatever groans there might be from his own benches, whatever abuse he might receive in the mails, there is little doubt that he was Labour's favourite Conservative, and rightly so. For on all manner of things he did agree with them. He believed not just grudgingly but ardently in such things as economic planning and incomes policy. Like them, he believed himself enlightened and, in the nicest possible way, therefore entitled to rule those less well favoured in a spirit of kindly paternalism. The spectacle of Sir Edward jostling his fellow Tories into progressive paths warmed the cockles of their hearts, for it confirmed them in the stereotype picture they had of the Conservative Party, as the guardian of the *status quo*, as the brake on the wheel of progress, as the stupid Party which they, the possessors of the true doctrine, had to drag kicking and screaming into the twentieth century.

In education one might have expected that Sir Edward's apparently oppressive sense of guilt about his advantages in life might take the form of denouncing Eton, his Alma Mater, like so many of the public schoolboys in the Labour Party, who are the keenest of abolitionists. But not a bit of it. In Sir Edward's case, by some strange transference, his guilt could best be expiated by sacrifice of the grammar schools. It was as if Abraham, called upon by a jealous Yahweh to sacrifice his only son, should instead offer to immolate his mother-in-law.

In any event, it was now his turn to be sacrificed (though he was not a reluctant victim: his political zest seemed to have gone) and he duly departed for the groves of academe, having been appointed Vice Chancellor of Leeds University the week before, and soon after was translated to the Lords. In his place there arrived a grammar school girl. She, by contrast, had no guilt sense at all and believed with ample justification that what she had, she had worked for, that in general talent and industry should yield their just return, and that the grammar schools were the ladder by which the bright, ambitious and assiduous children of the working class could rise in the world, as she had done. As she said five years later, when poised for still greater triumphs, 'The charm of Britain has always been the ease with which one can move into the middle classes. It has never been simply a matter of income, but a whole attitude to life, a will to take responsibility for oneself.'

Nor was this a case of generalising misleadingly from her own particular experience. On the contrary, only a short time before Mrs Shirley Williams had been proudly announcing to a conference of European Ministers of Education, that over 26 per cent of Britain's university population, and 35 per cent of students in all institutions of higher learning were of working-class origin. This compared with Sweden (long the model as far as Socialist progressives are concerned) with 14 per cent, Denmark 10 per cent, France 8·3 per cent, West Germany 5·3 per cent and Switzerland 4 per cent. Opportunities of advancement for working-class children in Britain opened up by the grammar school system were, as a matter of fact, considerably greater than in the Soviet Union and Hungary, where university places were hogged by the children of 'intellectuals' (i.e. middle classes) (see Tibor Szamuely, 'Comprehensive Inequality' in *Black Paper 2*). To be fair to Sir Edward, he had been overtaken by events. He was the epitome of the consensus Conservatism of the 1950s and early 1960s, which came within an ace of obtaining acceptance by the Labour Party. It was characterised by: first, Butskellism—that is an agreed formula for managing the economy *à la* Keynes on the basis of the Government guaranteeing full employment; second, an extensive Welfare State; third, a truce on the boundaries between the public and the private sectors of the mixed economy. Whether such a consensus could have long outlasted the 1960s, whether in particular Butskellism was not doomed by the rising tempo of inflation, must remain one of the more fascinating ifs of our political history. What is certain is that the death of Mr Hugh Gaitskell, the rise of Mr Harold Wilson, and the left-wing takeover of the leading unions, not to mention a majority of the constituency Labour parties, put paid to this consensus dream. Yet, as always happens, those who were emotionally attached to this objective, like Sir Edward, could not appreciate that the prospect of a cease-fire had gone and that it was more than ever necessary to man the trenches.

In education in particular, there had been a long period of

non-belligerency. After all, the foundations had been laid amidst universal acclaim by the Butler Education Act of 1944. That extremely wide-ranging measure in essence set out to extend the existing system which had proved its worth both in conferring literacy and numeracy on the mass of the people and in providing a ladder of opportunity for the bright working-class child. It was extended by the proclaimed readiness to spend more state money, by the inauguration of a large school building programme, by the reduction or abolition of such fees as remained within the state-maintained system, by the generous expansion in the numbers of university scholarships, by the raising of the school leaving age to 15 and by the promise of new facilities in the fullness of time, including nursery schools and county colleges. Yet the Butler Act sought not only to widen, but to deepen, to promote quality as well as quantity, to enhance not only the numbers of the educated but their excellence and variety. So it was that the Act stated that each child should be educated according to its 'age, ability and aptitude'.

On this foundation there was, for a long time, substantial agreement. Educational policy became to a large extent administration. The Party dog-fight continued, but the issues boiled down to how much should be spent and which sectors should be given priority. Thus, the biggest milestone after 1944 was the Robbins Report of 1963, which recommended a near doubling of the student population and a more than doubling of expenditure on universities, and this was enthusiastically supported by both major Parties.

The consensus formula of more money plus more administration (which means in effect extra work for the minister, plus more civil servants) might otherwise have gone marching on, but, in the late 1960s there came growing evidence that all was not well. The Butler and Robbins promises of more and better were not fulfilled. Mr Kingsley Amis indeed had said when the Robbins proposals were first mooted that 'more will mean worse', and, after only a few years of Robbins, the universities were in turmoil. If some of the violence was imported from Berkeley and Paris there was evidently a rich soil of discontent in which the revolutionary message of the Marcuses and Cohn-Bendits of this world could flourish and grow.

The criticism culminated, indeed one might say exploded, in the so-called Black Papers, produced by a number of prominent educationists, school and university teachers and authors who had watched the trend towards anarchy and falling standards with mounting anger. They obviously caught the educational establishment on the raw. Mr Edward Short, Labour's Minister of Education, seemingly humourless and self-righteous (but who nevertheless accepted a substantial payment of his expenses from T. Dan Smith, provided it was kept secret) went to the length of calling the day of publication of the first Black Paper in March 1969 'one of the blackest days for education in the last one hundred years'. This delighted the publishers, for afterwards it sold like hot cakes. Sir Edward Boyle responded with the rather strange, self-contradictory comment that the Black Paper represented an 'ugly backlash from moderate unfanatical middle-of-the-road opinion'.

In fact, though often polemical in tone, the Black Papers were extremely reasonable, and though the names of Mr Kingsley Amis and Mr Robert Conquest received most prominence, the bulk of the criticism came from people who were still engaged full time in educational work (as opposed to administration) and included highly distinguished figures like Warden Sparrow of All Souls, Oxford. No doubt their offence was to break with the consensus. What caused the rupture?

In the first place, they said that standards were falling throughout the educational system. The primary schools were not adequately doing their job of instructing their charges in the essentials of reading, writing and arithmetic. Sir Cyril Burt provided statistical evidence that standards in basic education were lower than they were 55 years before—Dr Rhodes Boyson has since capped this with evidence that they are lower than they were in 1870, when Forster's Education Act began the state school system. Another author showed that the academic performance of comprehensive schools was below par (any three good maintained grammar schools between them obtained more university scholarships in a year than any fifty comprehensives) and that, unless it was impossibly large, no comprehensive school with a normal unselective intake of pupils could have a sixth form sufficiently big to rival that of a normal-size grammar school.

As for the universities, the headlong pace of expansion led to shortages of staff, buildings and facilities. The story of student riot and disorder is too wearisome to relate, but, under the pressure of various forms of student violence, without doubt the whole idea of the university as the haven of disinterested scholarship and tolerance had taken a terrible beating. In reality the riotous student generation, did they but know it, far from being tough-minded, were showing an extraordinary degree of intellectual timidity. Many were, like Victorian aunts, terribly shocked that anybody (like, say, Enoch Powell) should actually say out loud in a public place anything which offended against their conventional (progressive) morality, and again like Victorian ladies, who put skirts round table legs to shield their nakedness, were so anxious that others should not be corrupted by contact with wickedness that they insisted on keeping it out of sight.

Thus, at a time when Labour politicians were starting to boast that more of the national income was being spent on education than on defence, the value for money had never been worse. Why had standards slipped so badly? The Black Paper authors were in no doubt: it was because of the ascendancy of progressive ideas of education which had conquered the educational establishment, were being taught as orthodoxy in the training colleges, and were therefore being applied ever more extensively in the schools. The basis of the progressive doctrine was that education was the means of reforming society and bringing the millennium, a millenium of equality, brotherhood and co-operation. Astonishing as it may seem, the progressive doctrine held that the innate ability of all children was much the same, and that differences of achievement were the results of different advantages of wealth, environment and family background. It followed that the evidence of differences which were the reflections of an unjust competitive society, like marks and examinations, should be suppressed. Again, in its extreme form the doctrine held that teaching was 'authoritarian'; children should learn reading, say, when they were ready. Instead of learning tables by rote they should play with coloured sticks or plastic blocks. At the secondary school level the ideal was the comprehensive mixed ability school with no streaming. At the university, students were to participate as far as possible in running their courses so as to make them 'relevant to life', and, of course, expansion took place in those subjects most 'relevant to life'—namely the social sciences. As a matter of fact, in many instances the social sciences' bright students were often quite right in believing that they knew more than those who taught them; but let that pass. The intention of the progressives is nothing less than to displace our culture and build a new, though scarcely defined, alternative culture in its place. Such tendencies are inimical to the traditional aims of education in a liberal society, which are to pass on the basic linguistic and numerate skills of our society and also the traditions of our civilisation.

The crisis of education was at the same time criticised from another, economic, angle, largely by the authors of the Institute of Economic Affairs. They pointed out that the Butler Act and succeeding legislation, by virtually nationalising educational provision—that is by, in effect, abolishing the payment of fees in the maintained sector—had destroyed the natural and healthy balance between the seller of the service and the customer. Instead, a nationalised monopoly imposed its will on the client. Thus the promise of the 1944 Act to provide education according to 'age, ability and aptitude' was on the whole a fraud. For parents, when wishing to choose a school for their children, came up against the Berlin Wall of the zoning system, which could only be got over by the minority of parents endowed with the diplomatic skills suitable for dealing with educational bureaucrats. The case was ˌsimilar at university, where, with generous grants (at least by the standards of the rest of the western world) and therefore approximately zero cost, the demand was invariably in excess of supply. Thus we had the dons in the autocratic position of choosing what students they would have and offering the courses and facilities which suited them. Student unrest may thus be seen as a means of obtaining by direct action what students cannot obtain as customers.

The answer, the authors of the Institute of Economic Affairs have long argued, is to restore the market in education. In schools this would come about by issuing parents with vouchers which can only be used to pay for the education of their children, but which can be 'cashed' in any school, state or private, which is passed as fit by inspectors. If this looks like an uncovenanted gift to the parents sending their children to private schools, this objection can easily be overcome by taxing the voucher. The result would be that schools would have to compete for the favour of their parent customers. Some would prosper and expand: others would shrink and go bust. The idea is not as bizarre as it may sound to many. It has respectable antecedents—it was originally put forward by Archbishop Bourne of Westminster in 1926 as a means of removing the unfair financial burden on the Roman Catholic minority of tax-paying and rate-paying citizens. It has also been shown to be practical and indeed to have results praised by both teachers and parents in a recent experiment in Alum Rock, California.

In universities, the market could be restored by abandoning

grants and substituting loans. This, it is held, would discriminate against the working-class potential student, but this is not obvious. At the moment, because the grant is never enough to cover all costs and therefore the student is dependent on partial parental support, the working-class student may well be more disadvantaged than if he or she were to obtain a loan which could be much more ample. Moreover, it is arguable that the need to pay it back later would be reflected in higher remuneration from the graduate's eventual employer. Indeed, the grants system is more of a subsidy to certain employers than to students.

This lengthy diversion has been necessary in order to indicate the nature of the controversies into which Mrs Thatcher was plunged when she was appointed Shadow Minister of Education. It is all the more essential to know this background because the Ministry of Education post was the only senior governmental office she had before becoming leader. It was also one which she held for a record length of time (at least for a woman) and which brought experiences which were crucial in the development of her character and outlook on politics in general.

Appointed on 22 October, Mrs Thatcher immediately waded in on the main issue, pledging herself to fight government legislation to impose comprehensive education throughout the country, and added that she wanted to preserve the grammar schools which had played an important part in their communities. What she did not like, she said, was the kind of botched situation they had in her own constituency. 'A condemned grammar school, and a condemned secondary modern school have been married to form a comprehensive.' Still, she was not against the comprehensives in principle and was not going to unscramble plans that were already in existence. Comprehensive schools were best for new towns. The posture was perhaps not so different from Sir Edward's after all—indeed it was bang on the line adopted at the Party

Conference, but the qualifications did not, as in his case, sound suspicious. Among Conservative loyalists she had that vital quality of credibility which Sir Edward over the years increasingly lost. She went down well with the newspapers too, and they were filled with friendly comments. The fact that she had two children herself was regarded as a plus; indeed the appointment had come as a bit of a surprise, but the *Daily Express* pronounced her a logical middle-of-the-road choice, calculated to appeal to Conservatives who considered Sir Edward too far to the left, without offending so-called 'progressives'. What did not seem to have been noticed was that Sir Edward was a friend of hers at Oxford and she was not going to go out of her way to say how different she was from him. At her Press Conference she had indeed been anxious to remove any impression that she was right-wing. 'I'm not a reactionary,' she said, 'you don't withdraw students' grants for rebelliousness.' The *Observer* gave her marks for having dropped her earlier attachment to flogging and for being violently anti-Powell. 'She obviously has her uses,' said Woodrow Wyatt's 'Who's Who' in the *Sunday Mirror*, 'Clever Conservative women MPs are scarce,' though he found her clear blue eyes 'more cold than exciting'.

In any event, the subject of all this comment was obviously delighted. 'It's the most important Department after the Treasury,' she told a *Time and Tide* reporter with evident satisfaction. In fact the Conservatives' policy, already formulated on comprehensive schools, was not an easy one to put across, because their approach was ambiguous. They wanted to be regarded as pro-selective but not to the extent of supporting the eleven plus because this was, they considered, no doubt rightly, a vote loser. Yet, standing on the rights of local authorities to decide for themselves was a formula not for stopping the juggernaut of comprehensive education, but for slowing it down. It was the same story as with the nationalised industries, where Conservatives were generally frightened of 'putting the clock back' and thus did little more than consolidate successive bouts of nationalisation. Similarly, if it were left to the local authorities to decide, then, when Conservatives were in Government, Labour councils would do their worst. This in itself would be bad enough because it often happens that local government voting goes the opposite way to the national. So local government freedom under Conservatives tends to mean predominantly freedom of action for Labour councils. On the other hand, when Labour takes power, even if the majority of local councils then swing back to the Conservatives, that is not much consolation, because Labour does not believe in local independence and readily takes powers to enforce educational uniformity.

Obviously Mrs Thatcher had to argue the educational brief she had inherited and, though it did not provide a really good basis of principled opposition, it is the duty of opposition to oppose, and, where principles are lacking, procedure is a good substitute, especially if one has a lawyer's training. So, in November, Mrs Thatcher made a big assault on Mr Short over teachers' pay. The teachers were tired of their shabby treatment by the Government, which was operating an incomes policy at the time, which meant that those unions which could put on the pressure through strikes or picketing would get more, while those in the 'responsible' well behaved professions, like teaching, were impoverished. Mr Short was an old teacher himself and was probably quite genuine when he said that he did not condemn the teachers when they took a piece of the strike action themselves, like everybody else. So Mrs Thatcher, on the eve of a strike by 4,000 teachers (though the total number striking over a period was about 1,000,000), told the Torquay Conservative Association that Mr Short's comment was 'very strange'. 'This must surely be the first time that a Minister in the middle of negotiations to which he is a party has condoned strike action which is in effect directed at the Government of which he is a member,' she said. As she

[63]

managed to include an attack on incomes policy in the same speech and still not say where the Conservative Party stood on teachers' pay, it was a very skilful performance.

In February 1970 she was back at work opposing the actual Bill for universal comprehensivisation. Mrs Thatcher argued (procedurally again) for delay between the First and Second Readings to allow proper consultation with local authorities to see how pupils would be affected. The real limitation on the comprehensive programme, which made it unlikely to be carried through completely for another ten, perhaps twenty, years was in any case the lack of finance for new building, though that made all the more relevant the Tory fear of 'botched comprehensives'—i.e. the simple renaming, say, at three existing schools as 'comprehensive' and putting them all under one headmaster. A deputation of more than twenty headmasters, councillors, school governors and parents from the National Education Association, which was opposed to the Bill and which went to see her at this time was very impressed. 'Mrs Thatcher answered each of our points very satisfactorily and was not satisfied with any comment unless it was backed by facts and figures,' an Association spokesman said. 'She impressed us far more than Sir Edward Boyle ever managed to do.' They had reason to be satisfied. Mrs Thatcher pledged that when Conservatives came to power the Bill would be repealed, and for good measure gave the same pledge, to huge cheers from the Tory benches, a few days later in the House of Commons. If one can't win the vote there is at least pleasure in winning the argument and, as Andrew Alexander said in his column in the *Daily Mail*, it was a tonic to watch Mrs Thatcher making rings round Mr Short and mocking the intellectual inanity of his case. Certainly she had a lot of fun with his explanation of how he would get rid of selection. What about the provisions in the Bill for special help for children with musical or dancing aptitudes? Would they not be selected? Mr Short replied that the Bill dealt only with secondary education. Mrs Thatcher then professed to be delighted to know that he was not against selection generally—a shrewd hit considering that Mr Short was such an egalitarian fanatic as to be opposed even to examinations.

Her general message to local authorities under orders to comprehensivise, or to direct grant schools under sentence of nationalisation, was now delay. To the latter, indeed, she said, 'Hang on if you can—we're going to increase your numbers when we get into power.' It was the only way, when parliamentary amendments (like the one she tried unsuccessfully to introduce to make the end of secondary school selection depend on the 'convenience and suitability' of school accommodation) were exhausted. Meanwhile the Selsdon Park meeting of the Shadow Cabinet on future policy came and went in early February. It was not notable for its ideas on education, which awaited a paper by Margaret Thatcher. It was mainly famous for generating the free enterprise policy which, when the going got tough, that allegedly tough man Mr Heath abandoned. Margaret Thatcher supported it though. As she said after the 1974 election, in the author's hearing, 'There is a lot of talk about Selsdon Man. Well I was a Selsdon woman.'

In March there was a splendid row about a Government Bill under which the mistresses and illegitimate children of university students would become eligible for grants. The students were certainly not doing much off their own bat to help their popularity at this time. Indeed one wonders if students realise how generally unpopular they are. A very left-wing Conservative junior minister told the author some time after this that he always made a point in any constituency speech of making a five-minute attack on students which unfailingly evoked a good response. In any case, in April, hard on the heels of this Bill to subsidise student sin, came a sit-in of students in Liverpool, following action by the University Board of Discipline to expel one student and suspend nine others. Mrs Thatcher's first reaction was to raise the question of whether there should be a revision of the law of trespass, and, while there was no question of introducing a special law for students, yet, as she told head teachers at a conference in Scarborough, the law should be tipped in favour of the moderate law-abiding citizen. Legal sanctions should be applied to those who took over university buildings and deprived the community of their proper use. Her conclusion was that the proper thing was to introduce a new crime, 'Malicious Trespass'.

The head teachers' conference gave her the opportunity to put forward her ideas of improving the quality of the teaching profession, her most significant point being that the salary structure would need improving to give rewards for ability and responsibility. The progressive establishment in education must really have been wondering what was coming next from this lady who could argue for both incentives for teachers and the maintenance of law and order in the same speech. What would happen if she became Minister? What indeed? They were soon to find out. To Mr Wilson (who is an ardent student of them) the public opinion polls were signalling that his best, perhaps his last, chance of going to the country was in June. And so he did; but when the votes were counted, seemingly against all the odds, and against all but one of the opinion polls, the Conservatives under Edward Heath won. That, if recent form meant anything, meant for Mrs Thatcher that ahead lay the biggest job of her career.

7

STATUTORY
WOMAN

Mrs Thatcher was at the Ministry of Education for three and a half years, but it was a time in which her reputation fluctuated enormously. There was a first period from her arrival until early 1972, in which she gradually became what the *Sun* newspaper described her as—'The most unpopular woman in Britain'. Yet thereafter, her standing, both popularly and professionally, both with the public and with the educational establishment, rose in a remarkable fashion. Certainly, in her first days at Curzon Street she managed to become the most controversial figure in the Government, and it was significant that the first division in the new Parliament came on education. This was on an Opposition amendment, deploring Circular 10/70, which ended the necessity for all secondary school organisation and buildings to conform to some comprehensive plan. This was a logical follow up to her withdrawal of her predecessor Mr Short's Circular 10/65, which *had* required local authorities to submit plans for comprehensivisation. What had irked the various representative bodies in the educational field was that they had not been consulted, and they were even more affronted when she dismissed their plea with the comment that there had just taken place (in the General Election) the biggest consultation of all, and besides, it was a policy to which the party was pledged in its manifesto.

The educational correspondents too were very put out. Sir Edward Boyle would never have done such a dreadful thing, they said, indeed, he had stated that he would not withdraw the Short circular immediately. Unfortunately, as the experience, especially of the 1970–4 Government showed, unless action is taken on changes of policy in the first few months, it is liable not to be taken at all. For somehow the rats get at all ideas which conflict with the conventional wisdom of the Department, and what seem to be perfectly rational proposals are overwhelmed by evidence to the contrary. Even in education, in the end the memo is more deadly than the demo. Still, Mrs Thatcher did push her circular through speedily and so the abuse began. One young girl reporter thought she was being very amusing in describing Mrs Thatcher as a woman who 'sounds as though she is always wearing a hat'. This was the mildest possible foretaste of things to come and, as the assault began in earnest, it was only a small comfort to have the support of the representatives of the secondary school teachers.

At this point, the Conservative Government was determined to reduce the pressure of public spending. Apparently Mr Heath was looking for £300 million cuts in spending by the autumn and the story was that £100 million were to come from the educational budget. Mrs Thatcher countered with proposals for reducing expenditure by raising the prices of school meals and cutting out free milk (in both cases ample exceptions being made for children of poor families). At the same time she kept the Open University at the cost of £3½ million a year and saved the building programme. Keeping the Open University was a sop to the educational establishment, though many Conservatives wanted to scrap it on the grounds that it was doing expensively and on a subsidised basis what was already being done commercially and with great efficiency by private enterprise correspondence courses, not to mention other well tried bodies like the Workers' Educational Association.

At this point auguries were still favourable. Mrs Thatcher might be considered to have done well for her Department, and she went off the the Blackpool Conference without qualms. Indeed, as John Grigg put it in the *Guardian*, comparing her with Sir Edward Boyle, while he went to the annual Conservative Party Conference as 'an annual purgatory', for her it was 'an almost effortless personal triumph'. The Bow Group, which at the time was in one of its most leftish phases, did its best to spoil any triumph that was going by attacking Mrs Thatcher in its journal *Crossbow*, and accused her of strengthening 'reactionary' forces in local administration (that is the people who were opposed to a uniform system imposed from Whitehall) by her issue of Circular 10/70. This did not bother Mrs Thatcher, who turned up to the Conference in a stunning striped hat, which was a real cartoonist's gift, and proceeded to lay down her policy without worrying a hoot about whether the programme was approved or not. She was going to give top priority to spending on the primary school building programme (a change from Sir Edward, who would have given priority to secondary education). She also wanted variety of choice in the secondary school provision and she would do everything she could to encourage the direct grant schools. She even said that if local authorities did not choose to take up places in these schools then she would attempt to enable pupils from that area to go by application straight there anyway, and finished up praising the valuable contribution of the independent sector. The motion was carried to the usual (for her) enthusiastic applause.

A third Black Paper came out at this time, which defended school examinations against the progressive urge to abolish them. Unfortunately the spirit of the Black Paper authors was not shared in the Ministry. According to Mr Ronald Butt, writing in the *Sunday Times*, there was already trouble with the civil servants, who were fighting a strong rearguard action to stop her plan for keeping direct grant schools alive where local authorities were hostile to them.

Meanwhile, Mr Edward Short, Mrs Thatcher's predecessor, when he was not shouting rude words like 'reactionary' and 'anti-progressive' (sic) at her in the House, was busy inciting teachers not to mark eleven plus examination papers! He even accused his former civil servants of being like Dad's Army. Certainly he was not a very temperate man, and in ordinary circumstances he would have helped opinion to move in Mrs Thatcher's favour. Unfortunately there were more substantial critics abroad. The National Union of Teachers had recently told her that they would not be school 'milkmen'—that is, they would not sell milk to the children on demand. Lord Boyle (as he now was), in his capacity as Vice Chancellor of Leeds University, made his annual address to his University Court and made a plea for an overriding commitment to higher education (the opposite priority to Mrs Thatcher's). Mr Jack Straw, the very left-wing President of the National Union of Students (NUS), in their annual Conference in November at Margate, said that a clash between the Tories and the student movement was inevitable, and for one session a member of the NUS Executive dressed up in drag to do an imitation of the Minister. In fact they ought to have been pleased, as the only action she had taken about students was to turn down flat the idea of student loans, which one might have expected her to favour. Yet it would in any case have been vetoed by Mr Heath. He had had a loan to go to Oxford, he told one correspondent, and he didn't like them. Since without the loan he would not have made Oxford at all, one might have expected him to have recognised the utility of loans, but clearly this was a case of unreasoning prejudice against which it was impossible to argue. In the New Year there was an attempt by the so-called Angry Brigade to blow up Mr Robert Carr, and there was a kidnap threat to Mrs Thatcher. A police guard was immediately mounted on her Chelsea home.

Mr Short appeared also to be tottering on the verge of violence, to judge by the language he used. In March, in his monthly column in the journal *Education and Training*, commenting on Mrs Thatcher's decision to allow Walsall, Staffs. to retain selective schools in its secondary re-organisation plan, he arrived without difficulty at the view that she was in favour of Britain being run by 'the mediocre 7 per cent selected on the criterion of wealth, not ability'. She was condemning a generation of Walsall's working-class children to become 'hewers of wood and drawers of water' and for their talents to wither and die 'because Selsdon Woman decrees it'. This was a level of argument which Mr Short managed to maintain for month after month in a most remarkable exhibition of almost Pavlovian consistency.

Then there was a row in April about a film called *Growing Up* which it was proposed to use in schools to teach young children about sex. The film included a short scene showing a couple copulating and one of a 23-year-old Birmingham school teacher Mrs Muscutt, masturbating herself. Needless to say, when the film was shown in a Soho cinema to, among others, Lord Longford and Mrs Mary Whitehouse, they did not receive it with raptures. Mrs Thatcher had to say, however, for such was the law, that she had no power to ban the film. It was up to the local authorities. Fortunately Birmingham City Council came to the same conclusion. The controversy did, never-theless, reveal that parents have no claim to interfere with sex education in schools; that, legally, our children have no right to retain their innocence.

In May, despite her successful recent efforts to increase student grants, Mrs Thatcher had her speech shouted down by the students at the Liverpool Polytechnic opening. Rather more dangerous as it turned out was the decision of the

[71]

Merthyr Tydfil Borough Council to defy the Government by continuing to give its children aged between 7 and 11 free milk. Other local authorities in Sheffield and Manchester followed suit. As a result it was necessary to put a Bill through the House to stop those authorities doing it. Mr Short was of course beside himself with rage, though he had himself, while Minister, abolished free milk for the children in secondary schools.

To make things worse, in July there was the proposal to make charges in museums. The idea was that this should raise £1 million, which the museums would hand over to the Government and then the Government would hand £2 million back. This eminently reasonable measure, which is in operation in most continental countries, met with a chorus of disapproval and prompted the Labour MP Mr Andrew Faulds to describe it as part of the Government's 'clear intention of dividing the nation'.

In April the school meal charges jumped from 9p to 12p and in July the press was full of the story that nearly a million children had stopped eating school meals. In September the National Union of Teachers were furious with Mrs Thatcher because she refused their request for a Government enquiry into slum schools. An enquiry she thought was a waste of resources which were better devoted to improving and building primary schools.

In the Tory Party Conference in October, Mrs Thatcher stoutly defended her decision to sell milk in schools, and condemned the Labour Government for making no provision for the medically needy and poor children at the time when *they* abolished milk in secondary schools. Yet even here her grip seemed to be slipping, and the reception was, by her normal standards, luke-warm.

Later the same month she received a memorandum from the Federation of Conservative Students which suggested that the student union representatives should be elected by all the students instead of being run by a militant minority, perhaps 2 or 3 per cent of their number, who attend general meetings. They further recommended that a Registrar of student union constitutions should be appointed in order to see that they conformed to minimum standards. Even the thought of this utterly incensed the student leaders, who, apart from any other objections, saw their jobs at risk.

In November Mrs Thatcher announced a £2 million increase in aid to the 176 direct grant schools to enable them to cut their fees. Labour MPs in a rare state of frenzy vied with one another to call Mrs Thatcher rude names. Mr Silkin smoothly dismissed her as the 'Minister of Lost Opportunity'. Mr Willie Hamilton distinguished himself with 'Mrs Scrooge with a painted face' and 'a reactionary cave-woman'. Mr Short ransacked his brain to come up with 'ideological élitist' which he fairly spat out, and, according to one lobbyist, a 10-year-old child in the gallery, who had come along to see the fun, turned quite pale with excitement.

The students had really turned themselves on by now. At Kent University Mr John Biggs Davison, a right wing Conservative MP, was prevented from speaking to the Conservative Association there. The Government's intentions, which had not yet reached the Green Paper stage (issued that is for public discussion) were, apparently, well enough surmised to be thoroughly unpopular. The particular suggestion which irked was the one that student union fees should be paid to the unions via the University administration, which would expect union officers to account for their expenditure. Under this scheme, in future, they would not be able to use the money for such splendid causes as the Upper Clyde strikers! So the rioting grew worse. At the presenting of the designation document of the South Bank Polytechnic at the Queen Elizabeth Hall in London Mrs Thatcher was mobbed by 2,000 students. There were mounted police there and two students were arrested. Fewer than 180 of the 650 students who had won academic awards stepped forward to shake her hand.

[73]

Some students walked out of the hall, led by their president, who had handed her two petitions. Six students, who were to have lunched with her, left before the first course was served after giving her a note which said, 'We have lived with the lies of you and your so-called democratic government for long enough.' Mrs Thatcher, unabashed, got up and gave her speech. As the Polytechnic's Director, Mr Viven Pereira Mendoza, was thanking Mrs Thatcher, there were chants from protesters being cordoned off by the police outside of, 'If you all hate Thatcher, clap your hands.'

As if Mrs Thatcher's cup was not full enough, there appeared in the *Sun* newspaper on 25 November an article entitled 'The Most Unpopular Woman in Britain'. It detailed all the usual things—Thatcher the milk snatcher, the woman who raised the price of kids' dinners, who refused enquiry into slum schools, the student tormentor. It stated that Mr Heath found her an embarrassment, called her a cold fish, said (as far as one can tell on the basis of no evidence) that she was an unpopular girl at school. Then it invited readers to write in and say what they thought of Mrs Thatcher. Dear old *Sun*! It was, as ever, so keen on female exposure that the habit seemed to have spread from the picture pages to the political comment.

In December even some pupils from an American school, the St John's Wood School, walked out on Mrs Thatcher as a gesture of solidarity with the British workers and against the Thatcher decision to stop the rebuilding of the Thomas Carlton School in South London—a strangely remote thing for them to protest about. Shortly after this the *Sun* made the great discovery that Conservative agents had been suggesting to some of their association members that they should write to the *Sun* praising Mrs Thatcher. A strange objection, since it was the *Sun* which had been inviting the letters!

While on the subject of letters, just before Christmas Sir Fraser Noble, Chairman of the Committee of University Vice Chancellors and Principals, wrote to Mrs Thatcher to say that his Committee rejected her proposal to make universities responsible for paying out the union dues. Public accountability was all very well, but they did not want anything to do with it: they had enough trouble with students as it was. In the New Year there was apparently nothing for it but to climb down: the students, or rather their radically minded leaders, had won.

Anyone less determined would have thrown in the sponge at this point and she does not conceal the fact that this was the time of her greatest trial. Yet her resilience began to show through in all sorts of interviews with women's page columnists who went along with their heads full of the latest nicknames and slogans—'the open refrigerator' or 'the ogre' or 'Salome' or 'Lady Bountiful calling on the villagers with a jar of calves foot jelly'—and found her charming and not in the least as they had expected.

The Opposition had wanted Mrs Thatcher's head on a platter, and as soon as they made this clear to Mr Heath his ingrained obstinacy and distaste for being pushed around came to the rescue. In any case, he must have reflected that if he was going to have a woman in his Cabinet (and as a bachelor he was in a way more obliged to do so than if he had been a family man), then, looking round the Tory benches, Mrs Thatcher was as good as he was likely to get. Also he was basically rather impressed by her, with her capacity for work which rivalled his own, and her firm will and steadiness under fire. The test came when the pack in the House of Commons started baying for her resignation, this time over her 'vindictive' interference with Manchester Corporation (who had been adding a dash of cocoa to the free milk and passing it off as chocolate). There was also a new Manchester plan to give children receiving free dinners hot drinks at the charge of 1p a week. Under questioning, Mr Heath made it clear that he would certainly not undertake to stop any further interference. It was a legal matter, he snapped. There was little doubt now that Mrs Thatcher was in the

Cabinet for keeps.

The new, confident Mrs Thatcher had appeared earlier at the dinner of the National Union of Teachers, where, according to Sir William Alexander, the leader of Britain's 164 education committees, 'Mrs Thatcher, looking lovely, as she always does, had proved beyond doubt that the Three Musketeers would have done much better with her help.' She was then kissed by Max Wilkinson, editor of the *Teacher*, the NUT journal, and the picture appeared on the cover of the next number.

Apparently some of the credit for this new and favourable development was due to a new Public Relations Officer—Terry Perks—who had come over from the Ministry of Transport and had begun his PR career at the Home Office under Henry Brooke, a classic example of the unlucky Minister. However, it was also due to Mrs Thatcher herself, who, on reading an advance copy of the James Report on Teacher Training, had managed to persuade the Prime Minister that, with this and the raising of the school leaving age coming up, 1972 was vital for education and that it was her job to see it through. This is why she looked so radiant at the NUT dinner: she had just won her point with the PM at Chequers.

It was helpful that in the following month a survey was published by the National Foundation for Educational Research, which showed that more than 70,000 out of the 850,000 children going into the secondary schools every year were illiterate. For this seemed to confirm Mrs Thatcher's priorities which singled out the primary school as the sector of greatest need. Even so it was doubtful whether it was new buildings that were required so much as a revision of teaching practices. As Dr Boyson and others were contending, the trouble with the primary schools was the neglect of the traditional teaching of the three R's in favour of progressive methods, which would only be successful, if at all, with exceptional teachers who were always in short supply. Indeed, unless something was done to remedy the deficiency, building more primary schools might have a counter-productive effect because in old buildings, especially if there are also large classes, it is necessary to stick to traditional methods. The effect of this report was, however, broadly useful to Mrs Thatcher because it put the enthusiasts for progressive methods on the defensive. The NUT, reluctant to blame modern teaching methods, were forced to lay the blame for illiteracy at the door of television—always a handy scapegoat, but not very convincing. Mrs Thatcher said that she and her senior civil servants were going to make an urgent study of the background to this alarming situation. It was the first step towards setting up the Bullock Committee and, if the portentous report of that body, when it eventually appeared, was a frost, it was good that the newer methods were being publicly put on trial.

Mrs Thatcher was now learning to outflank her critics. When she made the traditional ministerial speech to the National Union of Teachers' meeting in April, a hundred members of the left-wing Rank and File Group walked out, but the rest of the 2,000 delegates applauded and many of them stood up. She then gave a powerful speech, answering the usual criticisms and developing an important argument about the danger of factory-size secondary schools, and the need for comprehensives to be scaled down. There were no critics when she said she was going to turn down plans for monster schools. The greatest embarrassment Mrs Thatcher was having over her schools policy, indeed, was with some Conservative councils, like, for instance, Surrey County Council, which had the comprehensive bug in a big way and got frightfully annoyed because Mrs Thatcher kept turning down its all-in schemes.

When she talked to the County Councils' Association late in the following month, she promised to give her full backing to the teachers when they were having troubles with 'pupil power', a more youthful manifestation of what had been infecting the universities.

Even during the summer vacation Mrs Thatcher could not

escape controversy and, in August, she rejected a plan proposed by the Schools' Council for replacing the existing 'A' Level examinations grading, running from A to E and fail, with a new 20-point gradings scheme with an indicated unreliability of three grades. The Schools' Council, the Minister's official advisory body for curricula and examinations, which has the advantage of using Government and local authority funds to propagate its ideas, in practice reflects the views of the executive commitee of the NUT. Mrs Thatcher had, on this occasion, done her own consultation, and found that the proposal was opposed by the actual teachers who were closely concerned with 'A' Level examinations.

In October Mrs Thatcher was back on her old conference form. She told Conservative delegates about her plans for more cash for direct grant schools, polytechnics and nursery schools and announced amid cheers that she had saved 92 famous grammar schools from being turned into comprehensives by local authorities.

At this time the Conservative pay standstill was in operation and the London teachers were so angry about the stingy offer of £12 London Allowance increase which Mrs Thatcher made to them (the Treasury had actually wanted to make the offer only £1 and she would not even consider it), that the NUT lobbied their MPs and held a half-day strike. Still it was a minor example of how Mrs Thatcher was getting her way with the Treasury, even in the conditions of stringency prevailing as the Barber boom went into the sand. A more important example was the new expansion programme which she wrung out of the Treasury and which was set out in the White Paper in early December. Under it educational expenditure was expected to rise to 14 per cent of public expenditure in 1977, against only 10 per cent in 1962. The automatic response of the Labour Shadow, Mr Hattersley, was of course that the expansion was much too slow. Short of swallowing up the whole national income, one feels, it always will be.

Attention was diverted in the new year to a political dog-fight over some sixth-form conferences organised by the Conservatives in which Mr Norman St John Stevas, Mrs Thatcher's vigorous new number two at the Ministry, took a prominent part. He was hotly accused of infiltrating Conservative propaganda into the school curriculum. In fact it was not Mr St John Stevas's initiative at all but a campaign conducted by the Conservative Central Office and in view of the precedent it might set for when a Labour Government was again in power, not a very wise one.

From now on, with the lines of the educational programme settled and having priority treatment among the various items of Government expenditure, there was rather less tension in the educational world than before. Admittedly, the election as President of the NUT of Mr Max Morris, a Communist, did not help, and it was a pity that a visit to India prevented Mrs Thatcher attending the teachers' conference at which the previous year she had received an ovation, but which this time was addressed by Mr Hattersley, who had a field day without anyone to reply.

Rows went on of course about Birmingham's comprehensive plans being turned down, about whether there were going to be enough teachers, about radical students denying academic freedom to those whose views they disliked. There was an especially nasty case of LSE students attacking Professor Eysenck, a psychologist, for daring to say that Whites were more intelligent than Blacks. Professor Eysenck, ironically, had been similarly attacked for his beliefs forty years before, this time by the Nazis. Above all these discontents Mrs Thatcher presided serenely, and was now beginning to seem like a permanent fixture. She had long overtaken her forerunner as woman Minister of Education, Florence Horsburgh, and, unlike her, had survived the vindictive criticism from the left. Dame Florence they had called 'the face that sank a thousand scholarships'. Mrs Thatcher had had to take much worse, but there she still was, bright and smiling. In July there was a party at the Ministry thrown by Mr St John Stevas to celebrate Mrs Thatcher's three years as Minister. It was attended by Mr Heath, who spoke approvingly of a Secretary of State with very decided views.

What in essence were those views? Asked by the *Spectator* what she hoped to achieve in the span of that Parliament, she said she would like to feel that under her they had improved the quality of education, and were turning out young people better equipped to face life in society and to develop their own talents so that they should have some resources of their own. Later, talking to Mr Ronald Butt of the *Sunday Times*, she expressed her passionate concern for the right of parents to choose for their children the kind of school and teaching they, and not the educational establishment, thought best. These views were very much in tune with those of the authors of the Black Papers (one of whom remember was Mr Angus Maude, whom she was to promote to Deputy Chairman of the Conservative Party when she became Leader). Mrs Thatcher's difficulty was that few of her own party from top to bottom had any idea what the Black Papers or the Conference for Educational Standards were making such a fuss about. So, at the grass roots, there were Conservatives who had so far been brainwashed that as councillors they were supporting comprehensive schemes in the belief that this was outside politics. They did not realise very often that many of the advocates of comprehensivisation saw these new schools as instruments of social engineering. Mr Heath and his close colleagues again were anxious to avoid introducing free market concepts into education for fear of being tainted with Powellism. So this, as well as Mr Heath's innate prejudice, counted against the introduction of student loans or the voucher system—and it took a lot of courage for Mrs Thatcher to say a few kind and hopeful words about vouchers in her last speech to the Conservative Conference as Minister for Education in October 1973.

Another problem was the educational establishment, the teachers, the bureaucrats, the educational correspondents. Mrs Thatcher's disadvantage *vis à vis* these people was that if they took a stand it was always 'expert advice', however ideological in reality. When she took a stand it was 'political'. Civil servants in this country are still popularly assumed to be motivated by the highest ideals of public service and not to be self-seeking. It is not being derogatory to them to suggest that in reality their motives include urges for power and personal advancement very similar to other people's. Just as business men maximise their profits, so bureaucrats seek to maximise their departmental budgets. In aggregate they have a departmental policy and are like as not swayed by some fashionable doctrine. That said, consider the statement which the *New Statesman* attributed to Sir William Pile, Mrs Thatcher's chief bureaucrat: 'He is said to have stated—perhaps apocryphally—that although she arrived in the department with five facts in her head (all wrong) within six months he had succeeded in teaching her eight others (all right).' It is interesting to recall that Mr Ernest Marples said he spent his first six months as Minister in a struggle to establish who was boss—the Permanent Secretary or himself—and that was in the Post Office, not in one of the major Departments of State! Suppose then that Mrs Thatcher had been in conflict with her senior civil servants and had appealed to the Prime Minister. How sure could she be, at least in the first 18 months, that *they* would be the ones to go rather than herself?

Imprisoned therefore by circumstances, she fought a rearguard action for quality and standards and choice in education. She was able in this way to slow down the blind rush to comprehensivisation, and here her attitude tended, not unnaturally in view of her legal background, to be legalistic. In saving a school it was not the quality of the school so much as the number of petition signatures she received that counted.

Priority for primary school buildings was justified by their relative age and decrepitude, though, as we have said, that was not the only thing that mattered. Besides, the more money that went to primary school building, the less was available for comprehensivisation.

As far as milk was concerned, Mrs Thatcher was given all the blame for what was a Cabinet decision. Even that would not have mattered if it had been part of a consistent policy running right through the activities of the Conservative Government. Unfortunately, while saving millions of pounds on milk, the Government was wasting hundreds of millions on Concorde. In any case, the milk affair, which was not all Mrs Thatcher's fault, was something from which she personally suffered—she was indeed somewhat cowed by the ferocious campaign about it and she did not feel like taking on the establishment thereafter. She certainly went along with the raising of the school leaving age (though the teachers concerned, as opposed to the NUT, did not want it). She went along with the expansion of nursery schooling in deprived areas, though the latest American research suggests that this is a waste of public money. Nursery schooling does not improve the child's learning performance at a later stage. Nursery schooling amounts to a baby-minding service—why not then give a bigger tax allowance to mothers to encourage them to stay at home and mind their own babies? If the aim is to help children of deprived families, it is better to spend money on teaching deprived mothers how to look after their offspring and how they in turn can teach the children certain elementary knowledge. Within those severe limitations Mrs Thatcher did all that was humanly possible to preserve and promote the Conservative ideals of quality and liberty, surrounded though she was by zealots for equality and uniformity. And, more than that, like a true devotee of Kipling, she kept her head when all around her were losing theirs and blaming it on her. Moreover she was, from an early stage, right on top of the work at the Ministry and in the end her sheer competence and professionalism won universal respect.

Yet the time for implementing the White Paper's priorities was running out, not through any fault of Mrs Thatcher's, but because it was running out for Mr Heath's Government. Politics is indeed an endless adventure, and the forthcoming election and its aftermath were to bring opportunities and excitements beyond all expectation.

8

MRS
9½ PER CENT

Many leading Conservatives were convinced that a main cause of their defeat in the February election was the public belief that their housing policy had failed, and failed especially to deal with soaring mortgage rates. It was among the actual intending home-buyers, up to their ears in a mortgage or viewing the prospect of being so with dread, among, that is to say, the people who were the natural supporters of the Conservative Party, that defections to the Liberals had been especially marked. It was therefore necessary that they should make haste with new proposals to encourage owner occupation and to revive the old and trusted propaganda theme about building a property-owning democracy. That was why Edward Heath soon after the October election asked Mrs Margaret Thatcher, whom he had appointed Spokesman, to go away and work out a new policy. This suited her very well as she had no taste for idleness. June Southworth of the *Daily Mail* saw her at her Chelsea home a week after the result and Mrs Thatcher asked, 'Do I look bedraggled, woebegone, in a state of shock? At some stage I shall have to go to Elizabeth Arden to have the ravages repaired, but do you see the signs of shock in my face?'

Miss Southworth made no response, but Mrs Thatcher rather reassuringly answered the question herself, 'It's easier for a woman than a man to give up power because you are not so lost. I can fill the time by spring cleaning the house.' The main thing, however, was to find a new direction for her abundant energies and the housing policy assignment just filled the bill.

The Education Ministry was now well and truly behind her. She had no need to go back to her old office because, in her usual, tidy, organised way, she had never allowed it to become cluttered with a lot of personal things. Her former colleagues, however, were not prepared to let the occasion pass and on Monday 11 March 100 senior civil servants from her old department gave her a splendid farewell party. As one of them remarked, 'Never before had an outgoing Education Secretary been given a parting on this scale.' It was a welcome indication that she had earned the liking and respect of these professionals, and something to set against the malice she had endured for so much of the time as Minister, among education correspondents, teachers and students. Others would regret her too, notably those local authorities and those parents who were attached to their local grammar schools, which in many cases she had protected from absorption in ill designed schemes of comprehensivisation, and all the beneficiaries of the direct grant schools, for which she had raised the grants. Both were now to face a new onslaught from Mr Reg Prentice. He, like so many moderate Labour men before him, had been put into the Department of Education and Science as a sort of political virility test to prove his Socialism. In order to pass, it was necessary to swallow as many radical doctrinaire attitudes as his digestion would allow. Mr Prentice had evidently not quite realised what the form was and had got off to a bad start by saying that he was not going to do anything about direct grant schools for several years. Clearly the Minister was a slow developer, but after some intensive coaching in Cabinet and in Curzon Street he would come to realise that he couldn't go around saying things like that.

Mrs Thatcher was soon in action again when the House reassembled, this time in her new capacity as Spokesman on Rates. Inflation, now heading for 20 per cent per annum, was raising costs everywhere and nowhere more than in local government. This was partly because the disastrous Tory reorganisation of local government on bigger and better lines had opened up marvellous opportunities for bureaucratic expansion. The Tories had, it is true, made provision with a rate support grant to subsidise the domestic rate payer, but, when Labour came back to power, they readjusted the basis for distributing this grant so as blatantly to favour their own supporters in the towns at the expense of Tory voters in the country. This had results which even Mr Crosland, the new Labour Minister, felt constrained to describe as 'very rough justice with a strong element of the capricious about it'. Mrs Thatcher condemned this 'callous indifference' and pointed out that in some rural areas like Cornwall the rate would be up by 90 per cent. All she got out of Mr Crosland, however, was the promise of a thorough review of the whole system of government grants to local authorities. The main consequence, as far as she personally was concerned, was that Mr Heath asked her to take a searching look at the rating system in addition to her assignment on housing. This led Crossbencher in the *Daily Express* to write about 'Mrs Thatcher's rising star' as potential Chancellor, or even Leader, while the *Daily Mirror* suggested she might take over as Party Chairman.

Although the general ideas of the proposals for housing and rates were being floated piecemeal beforehand in speeches by Mrs Thatcher to various Conservative organisations—like the National Union Executive for instance—the formal unveiling of the whole package came on 28 August and served as a curtain raiser for the election, which everybody now knew was not far away. Indeed, Mr Anthony Crosland, when making his reply to the proposals, said at a Press Conference, 'Why rush this out just a few weeks before . . . .' He paused and the newsmen all laughed.

The main Thatcher proposals were:

> The Conservatives pledged themselves to bring down the mortgage interest rate to a maximum of 9½ per cent.
> First-time buyers were to get a 50 per cent bonus on the money they saved for a deposit.
> Council tenants of three years' standing were to have the absolute right to buy their homes at two thirds the market value.
> In the medium term, i.e. the next year, the bulk of the cost of teachers' salaries and 90 per cent of police and fire services to be transferred from local authorities to the Exchequer.
> Within the normal lifetime of the next Parliament, or anything up to five years, the domestic rating system was to be abolished and replaced by taxes more broadly based and related to people's ability to pay, but the local authorities were to have a specific independent source of revenue.

The proposals made an impact on the media and brought a furious retort from Mr Crosland, who dubbed the scheme 'midsummer madness'. He said that Britain was in the middle of an acute economic crisis and that the nation could not afford frivolous and lavish promises. He claimed that the housing proposals alone would cost £570 million a year and that the whole package would come to £1,200 million a year or 5p on the £ Income Tax. This savage outburst seemed at least partly provoked by the fact that they were being rather well received by the voters, and might make all the difference at the election. Many of the press reactions divided on predictable party lines. It was well received by the *Telegraph* and *Mail*, ill received by the *Mirror* and the *Sun*. It was no cause for astonishment either that the left-wing *Tribune* should say, 'Thatcher's vote-snatching policy is for the better off'. Still there was no moral basis to any Socialist objections that the plan favoured Conservative supporters, as the Labour Government immediately after taking office in March had frozen council rents—a blatant bit of pandering to a sectional interest considered to be mainly Labour. More worrying was the criticism from *The Times*, which was against all the proposals except that for first-time buyers. It argued that the council house offer was to those who had, according to previous Conservative beliefs, been feather-bedded too long; that the mortgage rate was an indiscriminate subsidy, which would inflate house prices; that to replace the rates (for which a previous Conservative Green Paper could find no satisfactory alternative) would cost the equivalent of the yield of the entire tobacco duty in 1973–4, or the duty on beer, wines and spirits; and rate abolition would weaken the independence and sense of responsibility of local councillors and remove the last check on waste. *The Economist*, taking much the same line, also saw a danger of centralising the wage negotiations of the teachers, firemen and police and thus making for a single national confrontation as opposed to diffused and less dangerous local confrontations. Mr Samuel Brittan of the *Financial Times*, Britain's leading economic journalist, saw the whole thing as an exercise in bribing people with their own money, and said that the proposals embodied 'all the fallacies of the control and subsidy approach normally associated with interventionist Socialism'. The 'prize for economic illiteracy', however, he gave to the 9½ per cent guaranteed mortgage interest rate, an open-ended commitment being made at a time of rapid and unpredictable rates of inflation. Indeed, it was this kind of holding down of interest rates which had caused the accelerated inflation under the Conservatives.

The interesting thing is that these proposals were out of line with the kind of thinking which Sir Keith Joseph had been recently outlining with Mrs Thatcher's keen support. They *were* an extension of the interventionist policies which were precisely what were objectionable about the previous Heath administration. As a matter of fact they seem to have been a good deal more *dirigiste* than Mrs Thatcher wanted, at least according to the Bow Group. Apparently their Standing Committee on Housing went to see her near the end of July. They had a long session with her, and indeed she was the only one of the front-bench spokesmen whom the Bow Group approached who gave them a warm welcome. Messrs Whitelaw and Prior had seen them, but had been reluctant to discuss policy or, for that matter, to admit that it was desirable to have any policy; they had generally been rather patronising, given them a drink, patted them on the head and sent them on their way. Mrs Thatcher, on the other hand, talked to them for hours and invited them to come back again. The interesting thing is that she told them that she was thinking of giving a pledge to stop mortgage rates rising above their present levels (about 11 per cent) but gave no indication of the 9½ per cent undertaking of a month later, at which they were all astonished. The impression which the Group gained was that the Shadow Cabinet had no policy except what Margaret Thatcher had formulated, that they panicked as the election approached and insisted on putting housing and rates in the forefront of their policy and, against Mrs Thatcher's better judgment, also insisted on the rather extravagant promise of a 9½ per cent ceiling.

It was certainly in the forefront, as well it might be, because the rest of the policy, especially the inclusion of a statutory incomes policy as a long stop, against the best advice, showed that Mr Heath and his confidants had, like the Bourbons, learnt nothing and forgotten nothing. It was certainly true to say that Mr Heath was a man of unusual character. It took a very unusual character indeed to decide after he had tasted defeat at the hands of the miners twice running that he would yet again embrace the policy which had already brought him down twice. It was understandable that, as this policy of economic and industrial suicide was all they otherwise had to offer, they should grasp at the one policy which had actually been properly worked out.

However genuinely convinced of the policy, Mrs Thatcher certainly defended it with gusto. In fact she exhibited, not for the first time, that bounding self-confidence which, admittedly, is in her case founded on a veritable mountain of facts and figures, but which in any case, and almost regardless of the factual position, moves all before it. So, before and during the election she appeared a good deal on television and, whether singly or in conflict with Mr Crosland or Mrs Ewing or whoever, always giving as good as she got and better. Was there any justification for this big subsidy to the mortgage? Yes, the statistics came rapping back, the average subsidy to somebody buying the house on a mortgage is £280 a year compared with an annual £900 which goes to the average council house tenant. Clearly if there was a possibility of swapping people from the latter into the former class it would be a gain to the community. Would that be the final effect though? The sceptic might reasonably say that the net result would be still more subsidised mortages as well as the subsidised council tenant we have already, and are going on creating.

At the heart of the Thatcher scheme, and this is where we must see the housing and the rating proposals together as a whole, is the intention of reshaping the property foundations of our society. The overriding aim is to put Britain into the league of Australia and the USA, where the spread of house ownership is much wider. Allow things to drift on as they are doing and the whole country will come to resemble Scotland, where the housing is overwhelmingly municipalised, and where the Tory Party is in dire straits because Socialism, whether it is national or municipal, creates Socialists. A property-owning or, more specifically, a home-owning democracy may conversely be expected to create Conservatives. For people are not likely to be Conservative unless they are conscious of having something worth conserving, and what is more worth trying to conserve in the polling station than a home of your own?

Of course, justifications of the policy were produced which in the excitement of election time seemed to pass muster, but which will not bear closer scrutiny. For example, Mrs Thatcher sought to make light of the rates undertaking by pointing out that the buoyancy of the revenue would produce an addition to the tax yield without any change of the tax rates, which would amply provide for the loss of revenue due to abolishing rates. Yet that is an argument which no Conservative should use. For the 'buoyancy of the revenue' derives from the combination of inflation and a progressive tax system under which, when inflation rises by so much, tax revenues rise by so much more, as people with higher cash incomes, but not necessarily higher real incomes, move into higher tax brackets. The 'buoyancy of the revenue' therefore is nothing more than a form of taxation without representation. For any parliament would think twice about increasing the tax bill deliberately to the extent that it would naturally expand with the present rate of inflation of around 20 per cent.

This argument was thus more plausible than permissible. Yet the underlying reason was the strategy of social power. This is not a fancy way of saying 'expediency', of saying in effect that anything was justifiable which would keep Socialists out. For that expediency approach is what has been so damaging to the Conservatives in the past, so that, though for a generation they succeeded more often than not in holding office, such has been their lack of conviction that they have mostly tended when in office to consolidate Socialism or even to promote it. Thus, especially since 1960, both the nationalised sector and the proportion of the Nation's income spent by government have grown almost continually, almost regardless of which Party was in power. Against that backcloth we can see that Mrs

Thatcher's fundamental idea was to back this collectivist trend and to steer the country away from the nannified, welfare-smothered, comprehensivised, council house community which is the apparent aim of socialist policy, and go back as well as forward to a society which honours endeavour and self reliance, and in which those who strive and save should have their just reward, at least in the form of a roof of their own over their heads.

It must be said, however, that Mrs Thatcher's rather rhetorical view of housing and its relation to the shape of society was incomplete, and this in a way sprang from the incorrect analysis which originally led to her being given responsibility for formulating the policy. For the real cause of the Conservative defeat in the February 1974 election was not mainly the defection or abstention of good Tories because of their disillusion with the Government's housing policy. This was an excuse and a pretty wretched one at that. The real reason, as every man in the street knew, and as Tory politicians were learning from public opinion polls, was the Government's failure to deal with inflation, and the additional inconvenience which its incomes policy produced when it applied to the miners to the extent of bringing in the three-day week.

Before pressing on, it is perhaps worth while to pause and suggest those conditions which would round out the housing and rates policy into a complete strategy. The hiving-off of educational, fire and police services should be seen not, as some critics suggested, as the beginning of a policy of greater concentration of power in Whitehall, but paradoxically as the reverse. Nor should short-term rate support do more than offset the effects of inflation and the imposition of extra duties on councils by the central government. It should not shield the councils from the anger of the ratepayer at their bureaucratic extravagance. A rate revolt is just what local authorities should go in fear of if their spending is ever to be brought under popular control, or any control at all. The rate, therefore, if it is to be removed, must be replaced by a genuine local tax which is a palpably independent source of revenue, and stating that problem is a good deal easier than solving it. The remaining services thereafter should be either financed out of this local impost or the service should be run on a commercial basis and charges made with a view to making a profit. This is no place to enter into details, but they have been set out by Messrs Maynard and King in *Rates or Prices?* (Institute of Economic Affairs, 1972). Also, to those who argue that there is a danger of centralising education finance (and that this would provide an increased opportunity for the Socialists when in power to impose a uniform system), the answer is that the right method of devolution is to the market-place and not to the local authority.

To return to housing: if council houses are to be sold off at a one-third discount the implication is that local authority building should be phased out almost completely (there would remain some special requirements like old people's homes) for it is crazy to build in order to sell at 33 per cent below the market price. It would be much better for people to buy direct from the private builder, who can in any case build cheaper than the council. The other logical implication of the policy taken as a whole is that councils should charge realistic rents in order to give people an incentive to own their houses. This might be carried out without social upheaval if the council house subsidy were given in cash to present occupants, instead of applying to the house or apartment, and lasted for a period of, say, ten years. The subsidy recipient would not of course be able to enjoy both that income subsidy advantage and the opportunity of buying a council house at a discount, otherwise some people would hang on for ten years before buying. So the initial discount would have to be phased out over the ten-year period. All this is a diversion, but one intended to show that the Thatcher scheme was not to be thought of as merely an astute exercise in bribery, but part of a grander plan for social regeneration.

There is no doubt that the Thatcher housing and rates package was the most exciting part of the Conservative programme. The main theme of the election campaign, which was less appealing, was one of national unity in the fight against inflation. Unfortunately, coming from Mr Heath with his confrontation background, it looked remarkably like an invitation to bury party strife in order to fight the unions. The best thing to be said for this campaign is that, combined with the Thatcher package, it succeeded in upstaging the Liberals, who might otherwise have stolen a lot of Conservative votes. As it was, the election result, giving the Socialists an overall majority of five, could have been much worse. Mrs Thatcher's own majority was reduced by 2,000 to 3,911, though her percentage of the vote was slightly up and the smaller majority apparently reflected the lower poll, the loss of Liberal votes to Labour, and the presence of a National Front candidate, who gathered nearly 1,000 votes, which presumably included a fair proportion of disillusioned Conservatives.

After the election there were many more disillusioned Conservatives who put the blame for this second defeat in a year on their Leader. There were indeed a number of Mr Heath's advisers who were anxious for him to go so that he could be rapidly replaced by Mr Whitelaw (whose popularity at this time within the Party was considerable) and then they could all carry on in their jobs as before. The leadership crisis could no longer be suppressed, and the usual press speculation began about a successor to Mr Heath. In the immediate aftermath of the General Election Mrs Thatcher did not even consider herself to be a candidate—except in the long run—and she told reporters that she did not think that the Conservative Party would be ready to have a woman as Leader for another ten years. Bernard Levin had said much the same: 'The male chauvinism of the people of this country, particularly the women, is still dreadful, and her sex would be a handicap.' He also suggested that she was lacking in warmth, the very quality lacking in Mr Heath, 'and there is no point in the Party jumping out of the Igloo and into the Glacier.'

At this stage (on Wednesday 16 October) the Heath office launched into the offensive (in more ways than one). It put around the message privately, first, that there was no acceptable alternative: Sir Keith Joseph lacked the necessary nerve, and Mr Whitelaw was a Heath man anyway; second, that Mr Heath feared that if he stood down there would be a right-wing takeover; and third, that though there was much disenchantment in the Parliamentary Party, people might still feel differently in a week or two's time, when they came to think seriously about a successor. Scarcely anybody mentioned Mrs Thatcher except in a throwaway line. The *Observer* on 20 October said, 'if winning battles in the House is the chief criterion, that might lead to choosing someone like Mrs Margaret Thatcher as leader, but she would be inappropriate in almost every other respect.' That or something like it seemed to be a very general view. Ladbroke's was offering odds against her of 50 to 1. In the next few weeks these odds were to shorten dramatically.

·

9

BREAKTHROUGH
ON
THE BUDGET

No single factor exerted a more positive influence on Margaret Thatcher's emergence as Leader than her dispatch-box duel with Labour's Chancellor, Denis Healey. For it was here that she exhibited a sharpness of mind, a grasp on the most complex, but also the most crucial political subject—namely public finance; and a forcefulness as a debater which, as a combination, were unrivalled on the Conservative front bench. This episode is so important and so revealing that it deserves separate treatment.

It all arose out of the difficulties which Mr Heath had in forming his Shadow Cabinet. Having decided obstinately to stay on as Leader he found himself in a quandary. The most suitable choice on grounds of experience and ability was Sir Keith Joseph. What disqualified him from Mr Heath's point of view was the fact that he had been the arch critic of the Heath financial policies, in particular the profligate increase in the money supply which he had embarked upon in his frantic pursuit of economic growth and which Sir Keith had identified as the main source of inflation: worse still, Sir Keith was, at this time, considered the main rival for the leadership. The choice therefore fell on Mr Robert Carr, a decent, amiable man, a keen Heath supporter, and, on economic affairs, on the left of the party (that is lacking enthusiasm for free market capitalism) but, alas, no human computer when it came to economic and financial matters. Besides, the prospect of two Finance Bills with major new legislation, and the need to have somebody putting the Party's economic case in the debate in the run up to the referendum, was too great a burden for one man. Mr Carr was therefore not in the least averse to the suggestion that he should have the support of another Shadow, even one whose economic philosophy differed from his own, because she was blessed with an expertise born both of her training as a tax lawyer and of natural aptitude and flair. Choosing Mrs Thatcher for this post looks in retrospect to have been Mr Heath's largest single error, because it gave her such an opportunity to shine, and it is interesting to speculate why he committed it. Basically, it seems to have been due to his consistent under-estimate of her political weight. Perhaps he could never seriously think of her except as the chit of a girl she was when he first knew her, who could not possibly constitute a threat to him. Perhaps it was simply that (except in the case of Sir Keith who had, in effect, already thrown down the gauntlet) he could not, after being Leader for ten years, believe that any rival represented any real danger. Except for Sir Keith, virtually all the leading figures in the Shadow Cabinet owed their places to his preference, and none of them apart from Sir Alec, who had just retired, and Lord Hailsham, who was not any more a contender for the leadership, had the standing and position which meant that they absolutely *had* to be included. This arrogance, or male chauvinism, or simple misjudgment more likely, was now to cost him dear.

There was the less excuse for overlooking Mrs Thatcher's qualities because she had been on particularly good form in the House on Guy Fawkes Day a few days before the announcement, when, as Norman Shrapnel put it in the

Guardian, 'She doused Michael Foot's chariot of fire by pouring cold facts on his head until he might have been expected to howl for mercy.' Shrapnel went on, 'It was a stalwart, capable performance . . . . We never get less from her and it would be greedy to expect more. She is also reasonably fire-proof.'

On the same day that they published the news that Margaret Thatcher was to run in tandem with Mr Robert Carr as Shadow Chancellor, the newspapers also carried a report of her speech to the Institute of Directors. There she descanted on the cash-flow problems (acute since Mr Healey's first Budget), defended free enterprise against the charge that it was begging for Government money, when in fact the Government was going to take £3,265 million out of private industry in Corporation Tax, and insisted that if it was accountability that people wanted then 'surely Marks and Spencers are just as accountable to the public as British Railways—and they put tax in instead of taking subsidies out'.

She now got down to work. 'I'm a very good night worker,' she said threateningly to Mr Denis Healey in a later debate, and she evidently was and is, having a Heath-like capacity for devouring briefs of great complexity. Unlike Mr Heath, though, on the occasion of what she recognises as a big speech, she has an ability to concentrate on every sentence and to work and rework every passage until it is right. Mr Anthony Wedgwood Benn, even when at Oxford, where he was her contemporary, was perhaps an extreme example of the technique, for even when getting ready for an appearance at the Union Debating Society he would, so it is said, give an hour's preparation to every minute of his speech. It is such single-mindedness which succeeds in every walk of life, and single-mindedness is what Mrs Thatcher has long possessed to a marked degree.

Her power of dealing with complications was now needed more than ever, for much had happened in the fiscal field. In March Mr Healey brought in his first Budget with an emphasis on swingeing increases in Corporation Tax. He was, it appeared, determined to reduce the money supply all right—by grabbing industry's cash (at a time when stock financing problems were becoming severe), thus driving large numbers of firms towards bankruptcy. He also announced, to left-wing cheers, his forthcoming Wealth and Gifts taxes. By July, with the dawning realisation of what he had done, he was back on the reflationary tack, seeking to mitigate the impact of his ruinous combination of inflation and controls, and generally repair the damage he had inflicted in March. So, while his preoccupation in July was (with the election in mind) to hand back his politically ill-timed increases in consumer taxes, in the November budget he was eager to restore the money he had filched from the companies. He also raised the charges of the nationalised industries, which had been kept down, as part of Mr Heath's attempt to hold the price line, but this had meant they went heavily into the red, a situation from which they could only be rescued by a subsidy from the taxpayer. In making the nationalised sector operate on realistic prices Mr Healey was doing what the Tories had originally been in favour of, that is to behave commercially. Mr Healey's speech was, by common consent, a good one and as we have seen it was not an especially easy one for the Conservatives to criticise. The task, difficult because it has to be done off the cuff, fell in the first place as is customary to the Leader of the Opposition, Mr Heath, who made a good, workmanlike, if slightly carping speech, making much of the Chancellor's refusal to say precisely what effect his petrol tax increases would have on a gallon of petrol, but, for all that, driving home the point that Mr Healey was only repairing the damage he had himself done. The same theme was pursued in more detail in Mr Robert Carr's speech the following day. He was sensible, sane, but unexciting. On the third and final day the debate was led off by the Chancellor of the Duchy of Lancaster, Mr Harold Lever. He was, and remains, if one may put it that way, the best sort of

Socialist millionaire. Indeed he is so sensible about so many things that it is a great puzzle as to how he ever came to be in the Labour Party at all. Certainly, from a business point of view, he is the best front the Socialists possess, especially as he is literate in financial matters in a way that Mr Healey will never be. He predictably made a bright witty speech, teasing Mr Heath, who, he said, when Prime Minister had 'reversed the usual concept. He thought it was the people who had to please the Government, not the Government who had to please the people.' He then went on to talk constructively about difficulties of stock financing, which Labour was taking in hand but which Conservatives had neglected, and enthused optimistically about Labour's brand new institution FFI (Finance for Industry) which would put everything right.

Now it was Mrs Thatcher's turn. She began with a reference to Harold Lever, who, the last time they were opponents, she said, used to take her into a quiet corner in the House to give her a little financial homily. One thing she remembered from these tutorials was that 'he always had a borrowing answer to every problem. I always felt I could never rival him at the Treasury, because there are four ways of acquiring money, to make it, to earn it, to marry it, and to borrow it. He seems to have experience of all four.' She complimented him on his skill when discussing rival theories on stock taking 'in coming down on both sides of the argument. It is a skill which should stand him in good stead at Cabinet meetings.' She felt that he was the statutory moderate in his Cabinet as she had been the statutory woman in hers. In talking next about the FFI she hoped it would not interfere with insurance companies so that they were obliged to forget that their first duty was to look after their beneficiaries. Mr Atkinson, one of the members of the left-wing Tribune Group, immediately got up and asked whether the same principle did not also apply to Trade Unions, whom the Conservatives accused of ignoring the national interest. 'With respect,' said Mrs Thatcher, 'I was speaking on the basis of a legal contract, not a social contract. The two are quite different things as the Hon. Gentleman knows.' Mr Atkinson insisted that if there was morality in law they should equate, to which Mrs Thatcher replied, 'Perhaps the Hon. Gentleman could equate them by making his contract legal as well.' This was a shrewd dig, because the last thing the Labour left wants is to legislate, for that would mean returning to the rocks and shoals of a statutory incomes policy.

Mr Atkinson duly quelled, she sped on, referring to the fact that in fifteen years of listening to Budget speeches, she had never known a Chancellor take so long to communicate so little. She noted the suggestion that penalties might be inflicted on companies which went beyond the Social Contract but without any similar penalty on the nationalised industries. She found it odd that 'employers are not parties to the Social Contract, yet they are the people who suffer the penalty if the Social Contract fails', yet 'those who are parties to the Social Contract seem to suffer no penalties at all.' She proceeded to argue, expertly, that price control concessions would not help profits. She made a plea for the small business to be relieved from Capital Transfer Tax, else, under the Healey proposals, they would become one-generation affairs. Then she came to Savings. The Chancellor 'never hesitates to penalise those who save. He had to have one vindictive bit in the Budget—the surcharge on savings income.' She quoted what Mr Healey had said to a journalist: 'I never save. If I get any money I go out and buy something for the house.' Mr Healey, very put out, denied saying any such thing, and asked her source. She referred him to the *Sunday Telegraph*. Mr Healey again denied that he ever made such a preposterous remark. At this Mrs Thatcher said she was very pleased that he was in favour of thrift. 'The Rt. Hon. Gentleman had better take lessons on how to invest from the Chancellor of the Duchy of Lancaster . . . . I am delighted that the Chancellor is a jolly good saver. I know he believes in buying houses in good Tory areas.'

She now turned to a tricky technical point about fiscal drag being negative, used a maze of figures and facts to cast doubt on the Chancellor's public expenditure cuts, and found the Chancellor 'woolly' on financing the borrowing requirement, once again brushing aside Mr Atkinson, who put what he must have thought was a frightfully clever question, and finally accused the Chancellor of failing in his duty. He had given the people no warning of what lay ahead, trying instead to blind everybody with complications and statistics. Yet there was a series of shocks to come—first the petrol price increases, second, the nationalised price increases, third, price increases due to cuts, and last, in April, increases in taxation and rates due to increased public expenditure. It was a case of 'sacrifice by instalments', she said bitingly. 'The people were ready. The Chancellor was not. He and they will regret it.'

It was a triumph. The shafts of wit, the rhetorical skill, the mastery of argument, the easy command of detail, the technical competence, the trouncing of the questioners, the sheer bouncing bulldozing confidence of it all, gave a lift to Tory hearts which they had not known for many a day. The press, too, greeted her performance with acclaim. Frank Johnson, in the *Daily Telegraph*'s parliamentary sketch, said that, 'She became the first Tory front-bencher in this Parliament to win from the Tory back-benchers a cheer prompted by enthusiasm, rather than by hope of distant knighthoods or peerages.' He concluded with the comment that, while not questioning her undoubted femininity, 'the Tories need more men like her'.

This seemed to be a widespread view. The leadership race was now moving into its stride. On the 21st, the 1922 Committee met, and apparently Patrick Cormack and some other Tory MPs there urged that the Party leadership election should take place at once, instead of in the following year under the rules being concocted by Sir Alec's Committee. This idea, while it obviously reflected a mood, had no practical outcome. More important was the fact that Sir Keith Joseph had finally decided that he was not throwing his hat into the ring, and a number of his supporters were therefore turning to Mrs Margaret Thatcher who had let it be known that she would only enter the contest provided that Sir Keith did not. The newspapers on Sunday 24 November had the story that she had decided to stand. The stage was now set for the final act in the Tory leadership drama.

10

EXIT
MR HEATH

On the Monday after the announcement that Mrs Thatcher was entering the leadership contest, the *Daily Mail* published an interview with their chief political correspondent, Gordon Greig, headed 'Why I believe I have to fight Ted'. First there was the decision of Sir Keith Joseph (whom she had strongly supported) not to stand for family reasons. As she commented, sympathetically, privacy was enormously important, and publicity can disrupt the harmony of family life, but her own children were now grown up and her husband had been marvellous and wanted her to stand if that was what she wanted. So, with Keith standing down, she felt it was vital that the Party should be given a choice. Besides, she had, when a Minister, been telling women teachers that they must apply for headship posts when they occurred. She used to say, 'You cannot go so far up the ladder, and then not go to the limit, just because you are a woman.' As Greig pointed out, she was ignoring her own earlier advice that no one should go for the top job without first going through the mill at the Foreign Office, Home Office and the Treasury. Perhaps she remembered the friendly counsel which they gave her at Dartford when she wondered whether she was too young to be a candidate and they reminded her of William Pitt the Younger, who was Prime Minister at the age of 24.

Almost immediately a storm broke around her ears. She had had an interview with a magazine for old age pensioners called *Pre-retirement Choice* and had offered the friendly suggestion that they should keep a store of tinned foods and add to it by buying special offers as a safeguard in case of need in inflationary times, as she did herself. This harmless and kindly proposal was immediately jumped on by all sorts of people, belonging to the moral indignation brigade. Mrs June Wall, a Committee member of the Consumer Association, expressed her 'disgust' at this hoarding: 'It is just greed. Only the rich can afford to hoard food or have enough space to stock-pile.' Mr Dennis Skinner, a Labour MP, accused her of filching tins of salmon from the pensioners' mouths and went on to urge the Chancellor to include the hoarding of large stocks of food in his Wealth Tax proposals. Mrs Thatcher retorted that what she had recommended was simply sensible buying for a housewife when the pound in her purse was shrinking. The *Evening News* took a picture of her store cupboard and it looked very modest indeed. Even so, Mrs Thatcher said that she would keep quiet in future and stick to her brief as front-bench Spokesman on Financial and Economic Policy. There were some compensations. According to *The Times* 'Diary', ever since she threw her hat in the ring, the Thatchers had been receiving an unusual number of invitations to dinner.

As Patrick Cosgrave pointed out in the *Spectator* at the time, the whole larder incident had a very contrived air about it. For instance, a Mr Tallis rang a radio chat show saying that Mrs Thatcher had tried to buy large quantities of sugar from his shop in the Finchley Road during the sugar shortage, but he had refused her. Actually, this was a total fabrication. Mrs Thatcher rarely shopped in the Finchley Road and she could not in any case have bought sugar from Mr Tallis because he did

not trade there. There was little doubt in Fleet Street that the
Central Office machine, or some part of it, was being used in
the leadership crisis, both positively and negatively; positively
to suggest that there was strong support for Mr Heath among
the followers of the party in the country, and negatively in
avoiding any defence of either Mrs Thatcher or Sir Keith
Joseph. Mr Heath, it is true, maintained throughout the
leadership contest an attitude of aloof detachment, of making
no speeches, of being above the struggle. Some of his minions,
however, were apparently less punctilious about what they did
on his behalf.

On 17 December, the Home Committee, which had been set
the task of devising a procedure for the leadership election,
came out with its report. The sequence of events was to be as
follows:

1 There should be an election within 28 days of every new
   session and three to six months after the start of each new
   Parliament.
2 Only Tory MPs were to vote.
3 To win outright first time a candidate would need an
   overall majority of all Tory MPs, not just those who voted.
   He (she) would also have to collect 15 per cent more votes
   than the runner-up. With 278 Tories in the House this
   meant that Mr Heath would have to collect at least 140
   votes *and* be 42 votes ahead of his nearest rival.
4 If no one qualified there would be a second ballot a week
   later and open to anyone, newcomers included. This time
   anyone with 140 votes or more would win.
5 If there was still no result, the top three names would go
   into a final ballot two days later.
MPs would then vote for a first and second choice—and, by
process of transferring votes, the winner would emerge.

One interpretation of these rules was that they provided a

means of having a vote of confidence in the existing leader in the first ballot and a free for all thereafter. Some saw it simply as a 'Coward's Charter', well suited to those who wished to push themselves forward for the leadership but afraid to challenge the present incumbent. From those who felt this way Mrs Thatcher received full marks for being prepared to take the plunge, and after all risk her political career; for Mr Heath, although he was to say, generously enough, that Mrs Thatcher was his top woman to whom he would certainly offer a post after the leadership election, might, in the event, find it hard to forgive and even harder to forget such an affront to his authority. He was indeed at this time having the Central Office cleared of all but his vassals, and it is difficult to believe that the same would not have applied, after perhaps a dust-settling interval, to his Shadow Cabinet.

Mrs Thatcher took things calmly. Besides, she had plenty to do in her role as watch-dog on the Finance Bill, and the same papers which announced the new rules issued an account of her slashing attack on Mr Joel Barnett, Chief Secretary of the Treasury.

There was one piece of good news on the same date—*Crossbow,* the journal of the Conservative Bow Group (which had earlier acquired a reputation for being interventionist on economic affairs and being generally on the left of the Party) came out with a demand that, for the sake of Party unity, Mr Heath should stand down. This must have been something of a blow for Mr Heath, as he would on past form have expected to receive the Bow Group's endorsement. What perhaps he was not fully aware of was that the leading figures in the Group, like Peter Lloyd, Peter Lilley and Patricia Hodgson, had turned monetarist, and one of their recent Queen's Gate Papers had been written by, among others, Britain's leading monetarist Alan Walters, Sir Ernest Cassel Professor of Economics in London University and the LSE. On the other hand, Mr Heath received the support of the Greater London

Young Conservatives an extremely active and left-wing group of activists, but they were not widely popular with the rest of the Party, nor indeed with the other Young Conservatives because of their rather noisy pursuit of Party offices, and their barrack-room lawyer approach to Party business.

And so to Christmas, and on the day after Boxing Day another article by Mrs Thatcher appeared in the magazine *Pre-Retirement Choice* in which she said that she expected to stay in politics another fifteen to twenty years and then retire. In the article she ruminated about what recreations she would have. One of her recent hobbies was collecting small pieces of Derby and Worcester porcelain and she thought she might take up book-binding and bind the thirty volumes of Kipling she had at home which were starting to fall to pieces. Strange to relate no one rose at this time to denounce her for stealing the bindings off the pensioners' claim books, and indeed the bad image Mrs Thatcher had acquired from the earlier article appeared to have faded.

Many of the other prospective candidates for leadership were now in a quandary because they dared not challenge Mr Heath but were allowing Mrs Thatcher to make all the running. In one of his last articles and one of his most sprightly, the late Mr Derek Marks wrote in the *Daily Express* on 15 January about what he called the Tory Party's 'instant Churchills', that is, the large number of people who were standing in front of the mirror and estimating their chances of being the boss. He poured scorn on the Tory 'champions' who would make their challenge 'from behind Mrs Thatcher's skirts'. Among the budding baton-wielders preparing for the next concert but one were found Mr Whitelaw and Mr Prior. They were of course Heath men, ready to follow their leader into the jaws of defeat, after which they proposed to turn back and see if they could snatch some victory for themselves. All the other senior members of the Shadow Cabinet were being speculated about, but the names being peddled around at this stage, though estimable people, were little known to the general public. They included Mr Richard Wood, Mr Hugh Fraser and Mr John Peyton. More important than all this was the decision taken in the third week of January about one who was *not* going to stand. This was Edward Du Cann, Chairman of the Tory 1922 Committee, the representative body of the back-benchers. Comment at the time stressed the role of Sally Du Cann, Mr Du Cann's wife, in persuading him not to go for the leadership, but there was another factor. This was a difficult time for the banks and it would have been very awkward for Mr Du Cann to leave his Chairmanship of Keyser Ullman when they needed him most. A group of Mr Du Cann's supporters now met and decided to throw their weight behind Mrs Thatcher. Another grave deficiency was repaired at the same time when Mr Airey Neave volunteered to set up an organisation to canvass votes. A great deal has been made of this development by writers of the inside story and indeed the public relations operation conducted by Mr Neave, with a team of professional PR and media men was very skilful and its effects were palpable, but the really crucial event was the decision of the Du Cann lobby to back the lady. This was the moment when the Thatcher bandwaggon started to roll, and if this was a piece of luck, Mrs Thatcher now proceeded off her own bat to add to those chances by her gladiatorial brilliance in the House of Commons. On 21 January she delivered a scorching attack on the Government's Capital Transfer Tax, which was indeed an iniquitous proposal. She castigated the tax on gifts and bequests as a threat not only to small businesses, but to all who worked in them. She accused Mr Healey of being the first Chancellor to put a tax on doing a good turn. 'You apparently do not understand the effect your tax will have on the lives of individuals, the economy, or indeed on a free society generally,' she said. It was a threat to charities too, she said severely, and on this point managed to squeeze from Mr Healey a concession. Finally Mrs Thatcher had her side cheering

"...the enemy, but, by God, she frightens me!"

enthusiastically when she promised to repeal it, except for its concessions to widows or widowers.

The next day was better still, for Mr Healey made the mistake of responding with a personal attack on his opponent, 'Mrs Thatcher', he said, 'has emerged from the debate as La Pasionaria (passion flower) of Privilege.' He went on, 'She has shown she has decided, as the *Daily Express* said this morning, to see her Party tagged as the Party of the rich few and I believe she and her Party will regret it.' The reference to La Pasionaria (a nickname given to a leading Communist lady from the days of the Spanish Civil War) was scarcely apposite, except that the original lady to be so named was a fiery orator. Mrs Thatcher certainly had plenty of coals of fire at the ready when she rose to reply. Of Mr Healey she said crushingly that she wished she could say that he had done himself less than justice, but unfortunately she could only say that he *had* done himself justice. 'Some Chancellors are micro-economic. Some Chancellors are fiscal. This one is just plain cheap. When he rose to speak yesterday we on this side were amazed how one could possibly get to be Chancellor of the Exchequer, and speak for his Government, knowing so little about existing taxes, and so little about the proposals which were coming before Parliament.' Then, with angry scorn, she rose to a climax of wounding denunciation: 'If this Chancellor can be Chancellor, anyone in the House of Commons could be Chancellor. I had hoped that the Right Hon. Gentleman had learnt a lot from this debate. Clearly he has learnt nothing . . . . He might at least address himself to the practical effects because it will affect . . . everyone, including people born as I was with no privilege at all.'

The effect was electric. Nobody, but nobody, else on the Tory front bench would ever have joined such expertise with such pointed wit and such savage disdain. No wonder the *Daily Mail* was carrying the story next day that her bid for the leadership was gathering such momentum that near panic had broken out among the Party's establishment. This was perhaps why at this stage its leading figures trooped out dutifully, one after the other, to say each his individual piece about why the winner had to be Ted: Lord Carrington, Mr Prior, Mr Carr. Great play was made with how Mr Heath had forecast economic disaster and that he would be proved right. This was quaintly beside the point because if the monetarist analysis was correct, then, given that the time lag between an increase of money supply and its effect in raising prices is about eighteen months, the disaster which Mr Heath was predicting was of his own making. Moreover, it was not so much a case of his being proved eventually right as being found originally wrong. It was like a man who put a lighted match to a house expecting to be congratulated for subsequently ringing the fire brigade.

The campaign was now hotting up, but at least some of the civilities were observed. On 26 January the press was full of pictures of Mrs Thatcher and Mr Prior in evening dress on the occasion of Mr Prior's fulfilling a long-standing engagement to speak in Mrs Thatcher's constituency. That same evening Mrs Thatcher paid a tribute to Mr Prior: 'If Jim came in I'd be happy to serve under him.' As the nominations for the leadership battle went in (Mrs Thatcher's sponsor was Mr Du Cann) the Heath propaganda machine now went to work in characteristic fashion, suggesting that Mrs Thatcher's sturdy defence of middle-class values would be a liability and would leave the Party with only a rump of support (especially given her limited regional appeal), confined to the middle-class suburbs of the South East. Yet, as Mrs Thatcher pointed out then and later, the so-called middle-class values of thrift and independence are to be found in all classes—people on council housing estates have no time for spongers. As for the decline of party support in urban areas and in the North, it was under Mr Heath that those reverses had been suffered. Again, the notion that a man from Broadstairs, and one who was the very epitome of what Robert Conquest has called 'South coast managerialism', should have more inherent appeal to northerners than a girl born and bred in Grantham was far from glaringly apparent. Then again, stress was laid on Mr Heath's special appeal to the country's youth by providing Young Conservatives with tee shirts inscribed with the puerile slogan 'I'm for the Grocer, not the Grocer's daughter'—a fine example of the dignified reserve which, according to some of the press commentators, was so characteristic of Mr Heath's campaign! Of course the Greater London Young Conservatives included some young people who could be enlisted for almost anything which looked vaguely like a demo, but the basic fact has to be faced that it was under Mr Heath's leadership that the Young Conservative movement, once alleged to be the largest youth organisation in the free world, melted away to perhaps 15,000 in the whole of Britain.

There was one more contender, Mr Hugh Fraser, MP for Stafford and Stone, an aristocrat, brother of Lord Lovat, and husband of Antonia Fraser the writer. It is still not clear why he stood, unless it was to attract those votes on the right, of male chauvinists and others, who could not possibly vote for Mrs Thatcher but wanted an alternative to Mr Heath. Much was made at the time of the disadvantage of having a woman Leader, but, as Mr Bernard Levin pointed out in *The Times,* on the day of nominations, the belief that a woman could not become the Conservative Leader was a myth comparable to the even more strongly held American conviction that no Catholic could become President of the United States, and as easily falsified here as in America when John Kennedy was elected.

January drew to a close with Mr Willie Whitelaw declaring his faith in Mr Heath, and Sir Keith Joseph making the equally predictable declaration that he was for Mrs Thatcher and, more interestingly, that he had only recently become a Conservative, though he had been a member of the Conservative Party for many years. This was because a true Conservative should stand for a social market economy, or free enterprise capitalism plus a social conscience. On 1 February the *Daily Mail* produced its own poll of MPs on the leadership contest and found that, though Mr Heath was leading, Mrs Thatcher already had 38 per cent of the declared vote, but this left the race wide open because 93 of those consulted refused to say whom they were voting for. At this point Mrs Thatcher made what was, in effect, her campaign speech. It was made to the Party officers in her Finchley Constituency and it was not released through the Central Office Publicity Department. 'Forget that I'm a woman', she said. 'Forget the accusations that I am a right-winger demanding privilege . . . . I had precious little privilege in my early years.' Then came the message: 'I am still trying to represent the deep feelings of those many thousands of rank and file Tories in the country—and potential Conservative voters too—who feel let down by our Party and find themselves unrepresented in a political vacuum.' As a member of it she took her own share of blame for the mistakes committed by the Heath Government of 1973-4. 'But I hope I have learned something from the failures and mistakes of the past and can help to plan constructively for the future.' She then gave an outline of her political philosophy, her concern for freedom and the danger of excessive state power, the right of the thrifty and hard-working to succeed and make provision for their children, the need to defend diversity of choice and private property (against the Socialist state), and the right to work without oppression by employer or trade union boss.

She added, 'There is a widespread feeling in the country that the Tory Party has not defended these ideals explicitly and toughly enough and that Britain is set on a course towards inevitable Socialist mediocrity. That course must not only be halted, it must be reversed. The action by the Tory Party must begin now.'

This was a powerful statement and it clearly showed that she was not simply an alternative candidate to Mr Heath but, unlike others who were waiting in the wings, she was offering a

genuine alternative approach. Would this rebound on her? Mr
Enoch Powell, speaking to the annual dinner of the Selsdon
Group (a Tory group which was founded with the aim of
steering the Conservatives back to the aims and principles laid
down at the Selsdon Park Conference of the Shadow Cabinet in
January 1970), set out to ensure that it should rebound. He
said, in referring to the avowals of the Thatcher supporters,
that she used 'to murmur and grumble a lot in private', that it
was not among 'private murmurers and grumblers, and disloyal
colleagues, willing to wound but afraid to strike, holding one
opinion outside the Cabinet, but inside acquiescing in the
opposite' that a new Leader would be found. It was all very well
to recant over Tory failure when failure carried no penalty, he
went on. 'It was then that those ladies and gentlemen were
found lacking. It was then that they failed the Party, far worse
than Edward Heath.' He concluded scathingly, 'Let us leave the
dead to bury the dead.'

This was a harsh judgment and came from one who had
certainly had the courage to resign himself, notably on the
occasion in 1958 when he disagreed with Mr Macmillan over
the latter's excessive spending. Yet he too had in office
acquiesced in policies of which, to judge by his later
statements, he must have disapproved. For instance, at the
Ministry of Health, he had supported both the import of West
Indian nurses, and the imposition on nurses of all colours of an
incomes policy. He was also at one time a keen advocate of
membership of the European Community and edited a CPC
pamphlet *One Europe* (of the One Nation group), which was
one of the best examples of advocacy of the policy of joining
then or since. He has said that he changed his mind about that,
which he was perfectly entitled to do, but did he accomplish
the change-over without any intervening period of anxious
doubts, accompanied perhaps by murmurings and grumblings
to colleagues, or did it all happen suddenly of an afternoon, like
St Paul's conversion on the road to Damascus? Besides,

The right choice

State Opening, 1970

Conference, 1970

Minister at home, 1970

Look and say

Law and disorder

Eastern Approaches, 1972

In command – after three years as Minister, 1973

Mrs 9½ per cent, 1974

In the boudoir, 1974

Politics in the family, 1975

Foot in the door – after the first ballot, 1975

Sweet smile of success, 1975

Thatchers triumphant, 1975

Brief Encounter – with Mr Whitelaw, 1975

resigning is a very difficult operation to conduct properly. Many, perhaps most, resignations are on the wrong issue. Ideally Eden should have resigned over Munich. In fact he resigned earlier over the wording of an agreement with Mussolini. Politics is an untidy broken-backed sort of activity and it requires great judgment to know when one should stay with the team and when one should cut away because a principle has been infringed. For parties are not only united, (if they are lucky) by something resembling a common approach; they are combinations of politicians who are pursuing power, and there will always be tensions between principle and expediency even when the principles themselves are beyond dispute. Admittedly, it must have been galling for Mr Powell, who was the original and brilliant critic of Mr Heath's collectivist policies, to find others who had earlier lain low harvesting the discontents of which he had sown the seeds. Yet that is all part of the life of politics, part of the injustice of life in general. For the sinner that repenteth has always been more likely to have the fatted calf killed for his benefit than the worthy fellow who has stayed on the family farm and milked the cow. As Mr R.A. (now Lord) Butler once wryly observed on the tragic disappointment of a colleague, 'He now realises that virtue really is its own reward.'

So the leadership contest steadily moved on towards its climax and, for the many who found Conservative politics surpassing dull over the years, it was quite enjoyable. Instead of damaging the Party, it made it more interesting, and the news coverage and comment it evoked in press and on television was so great as to provoke some Labour complaints. One of the most significant developments in the final few days was the decision of *The Times* to come out against Mr Heath, not in favour, be it said, of Mrs Thatcher, but of Mr Whitelaw on the next round. The first ballot, or so *The Times* leading article argued on 1 February, was to decide for or against Mr Heath, and it came down against him on the issue of inflation. 'In this essential respect', it said, 'Mr Heath is the least suitable of the three candidates on the first ballot; he alone remains committed to his own wrong policies. He was wrong and he will not admit he was wrong.' It concluded that, 'Mr Heath, whether elected or no, cannot offer a future to the Conservative Party so long as he is the prisoner of his own past.'

The *Daily Telegraph* did a public service by arranging for the leading personalities of the Conservative Party to write features on how they saw the future of the Conservative Party and its policies. Mr Heath amply justified what *The Times* was to say—that he had no notion of changing the policies which had earlier led to disaster and defeat. The essence of his philosophy of politics was pragmatism. The Conservative role he saw as responding to what the public demanded of them and keeping a proper balance of social forces within which liberty could survive. Yet he gave little indication of what the principle of that balance should be: in essence it was an appeal for a doctor's mandate to trust Ted. Mrs Thatcher's piece, all of which she wrote herself, was by contrast a straightforward but eloquent plea for the 'kind of Tory Party (which) would make no secret of its belief in individual freedom and individual prosperity, in the maintenance of law and order, in the wide distribution of private property, in rewards for energy, skill and thrift, in the diversity of choice, in the preservation of local rights in local communities'.

In the Sunday papers there was a report of another speech by Mrs Thatcher which argued that the Conservative Party was in need of the kind of leadership that listens. 'Our greatest fault in office was that we did not listen enough to what our supporters and sympathisers were saying.' We should 'Listen to the younger generation', she insisted. 'They don't want equality and regimentation, but opportunity to shape their world while showing compassion to those in real need.' She concluded that the Party's role was to listen and to lead.

This was much less interesting than the previous speech and might have looked to the wary like a last minute attempt to stop the rot. For it was starting to look as if the tide was running Mr Heath's way.

The Harris Poll, which appeared in the *Daily Express* on Monday 3 February, found that seven out of ten Conservative voters were pro-Heath, while, as an alternative Leader, Mrs Thatcher was trailing behind Mr Whitelaw. Lord Home, who had himself once been toppled by Mr Heath, showed himself as a man completely free of rancour by now pronouncing in favour of Mr Heath remaining Leader. On the eve of the vote the National Union (the voluntary side of the Party organisation) reported to the 1922 Committee that four-fifths of the constituencies were for Mr Heath continuing as leader, though many of them really wanted a wider choice. There was some complaint in the *Daily Telegraph* at this time about the way the Party machine was being used to further the Heath cause. With the recent partial centralisation of the agents' profession, there was indeed more likelihood than previously that the constituency agents would do as they were told, and, among other things, consult those people who were known to be favourable to Mr Heath while ignoring those who were against him. Yet it still looked from the Harris Poll as if the findings were substantially correct.

It now seems that these findings fatally misled the Heath camp and that they made the mistake of trying to hustle the MPs, who of course were a very different proposition from the Constituency Associations which included a lot of place-hunters and people hoping for honours (though Mr Heath had been singularly ungenerous in doling out the knighthoods). MPs, though self-seeking and ambitious, were more independent and more likely to be swayed by ability to win debates in the House and elections in the country, and they resented the attempt to put pressure on them from constituencies, especially when they thought that the job of consulting constituents was a job they could and should do for themselves. All in all the Heath men overdid it. They gave out to the media the confident news that they had done their calculations and Mr Heath was going to win on the first ballot. This was counter-productive with two kinds of people. There were, first, those former Ministers and others who felt that they had an obligation to their old chief to see that he was not humiliated, and so they were going to vote for him, hoping that Mrs Thatcher would do well enough to make a second ballot necessary so that Mr Heath would have the opportunity gracefully to retire. But what if, far from being humiliated, he were to win on the first ballot? Second, there were those who wanted a change of Leader, but no change in policy; they only wanted Mrs Thatcher to stop Mr Heath and then make the path smooth for the man of their choice. Both these categories were now alarmed at the thought of Mr Heath with a first ballot win, regarding it as a vindication of himself and all he stood for, which would make him more full of himself than ever. Again the count which the Heath men had made was probably faulty. Knowing Mr Heath's less than charitable attitude to those who opposed him, some gave assurances of support who had not the slightest intention of voting for him.

The Heath team thus played into the hands of Mr Airey Neave, who had all through the campaign displayed a remarkable sureness of touch. He had avoided any PR vulgarity and stuck to a quiet, softly-softly campaign of persuasion. Mrs Thatcher's performance in the 'World in Action' television programme also helped the process of persuasion. Mr Neave said later it gained 15 to 20 votes. Near the end Mr Neave apparently posted his team all around the Palace of Westminster with instructions to look glum. One way and another then the stage directions and the behaviour of the cast were conspiring to produce a very different ending from what the newspaper pundits were leading everyone to expect. Yet, when it came, even the inner circle of Thatcher supporters was amazed. For, when the votes came to be counted, Mrs Thatcher not only stopped Mr Heath, she had overtaken him. She had 130 votes to his 119, Mr Hugh Fraser had only 16. Within two hours Mr Heath announced his resignation. So, after ten years, the old Leader had been ousted by a woman. Yet the question was still open as to who should take his place.

11

VICTORY
IN THE
SECOND ROUND

Mr Norman St John Stevas was the first to bring Mrs Thatcher news of her triumph. Her sober reaction was, 'Now we have lots of work to do.' This was perfectly true. For many still saw her role in the election as that of a stalking horse, useful for removing the old Leader but lacking the qualities required for the new. Already the Heathites were forming up behind another prospective Leader whom many of them had wanted to take over immediately after the election. This was Mr William Whitelaw, the Chairman of the Conservative Party, a large, genial, ebullient landowner from Cumberland. He had been Chief Whip for many years under Mr Heath and knew the Parliamentary Party well. He had also been the Minister who had tried to introduce the Tory power-sharing plan for Ulster and, although the Ulster situation was in fact going from bad to worse, it was the received idea at the time among top people that Willie had done awfully well, and this view was faithfully mirrored in the media. Certainly, if energy and oceans of good will could have brought peace to Ulster, then by Mr Whitelaw it would have been brought. Similarly, it was argued that for a Party so divided against itself, the touch of the experienced conciliator was required. Mr Whitelaw's benevolence would descend like soothing balm on everyone and miraculously all wounds would be healed. In any event, within two hours of Mr Heath announcing his withdrawal from the contest Mr Whitelaw declared his intention of entering it. 'I have made up my mind that it is in all circumstances my duty to stand', he said. 'I can only hope that I might be able to do something to unite our Party.'

Meanwhile, at least one interim celebration was in order. At 7.15 Mrs Thatcher gave a reception at Mr Airey Neave's flat in Westminster Gardens. 'Part of me is a woman,' she said, 'and part of me is a politician. The MPs voted for the whole of me.' Anyway, she looked well worth voting for in all the press pictures, where she appeared mostly with champagne glass in hand and flanked by her obviously proud and delighted husband and son.

Two days later the Gallup Poll published its survey, in the *Daily Telegraph*, of whether people thought Mrs Thatcher would or would not make a good Leader of the Conservative Party. The poll was conducted practically on the eve of the first ballot, so it was unaffected by its result. It showed a majority of the voters did *not* think she would make the grade as a leader, and even a majority of Conservative voters did not, though by only a small margin. The interesting thing was that a majority of all women liked the idea of her as a leader and a particularly large majority of Conservative women did. This finding was in conflict with the usual assumption (shared as we have seen by Mr Bernard Levin) that the real enemies of the advancement of women are women. The assumption had to be that if Labour women were in favour of her being Tory Leader they must, up to a point, identify with her, and that could have profound effects if she were to lead the Tories in a General Election.

The second ballot was to take place the following Tuesday, so those who wished to stand had to put their names in without delay. It was thus only the day after the result of the ballot that the names of the new contestants were known. They were (apart from Mr Whitelaw) Mr James Prior, once Mr Heath's personal assistant (in which capacity he had, to his credit, tried to effect a reconciliation between Heath and Powell), a former Minister of Agriculture and Deputy Chairman of the Conservative Party. He was running on the same party unity ticket as Mr Whitelaw, though this was ironic, since one would have expected that they might have therefore been able to sink their differences and decide that only one of them should stand. There was also Sir Geoffrey Howe, former Solicitor-General, former Chairman of the Bow Group, sharing many of the market economy views of Mrs Thatcher and Sir Keith Joseph, but weakened from this point of view by the fact of his having been Prices Minister in the Heath Government. For he had been obliged at that time to stand his natural convictions on their head and make all sorts of unconvincing assertions about the compatibility of price and wage controls with a free economy. He was intellectually the brightest of Mrs Thatcher's rivals and bright enough to know he was not going to win the contest which he entered, mainly with an eye to staking his claim in the future. Finally there was Mr John Peyton, Shadow Leader of the House and the dark horse of the election. Yet, although a sharp and witty debater and with ministerial experience behind him in the last Heath Government, where he was the Minister of Transport, he was the least popularly known of all the candidates.

Mrs Thatcher was not able to spend all her time thinking about the leadership contest, she was still very busy leading the day-to-day opposition to the Finance Bill as it passed through the Committee Stage. The day after the first ballot she was in the middle of it, dealing masterfully with a very complicated amendment concerned with the Gift Tax and whether it applied to compensation money to terrorist victims in Belfast, which Mr Joel Barnett had so misunderstood that he thought a mistake had been made by the printer. Mrs Thatcher cheerfully explained the position until he got it straight and evoked a surprising tribute from one *Guardian* correspondent, Simon Hoggart: 'There is no doubting whatever Mrs Thatcher's remarkable ability for the kind of close detailed in-fighting involved in Committee work.'

On the Thursday another poll was published, this time from the Opinion Research Centre on behalf of Independent Television 'News at Ten'. This was good news for Mrs Thatcher because it showed that one in two women believed that women voters would be more likely to support the Conservatives with her as Leader. Especially interesting was the finding that nearly one-third of Labour women voters held this view. There was also a strong feeling among women that a woman was better able to solve the problem of inflation than a man. Finally it showed that hostility to Mrs Thatcher among women voters was very low.

Mr Norman St John Stevas, who had resisted many blandishments in the first round from the Heath lobby to declare for their man, now affirmed his support for Mrs Thatcher. He had been a close friend of hers from the time when he served under her at the Ministry of Education, and his support was very useful at this juncture because his appeal was to the centre rather than to the right, where, in the crude sense that this term has any meaning, the weight of Mrs Thatcher's backing lay. He was to be seen in the corridors of the House from now on, discreetly persuading wavering members to join the 'Blessed Margaret' and enter a state of political grace.

This was altogether a splendid time for friendly persuasion. One new young member said he wished the whole thing could go on to the hundredth ballot because he had never in his life had so many invitations to dinner. There was a worry though among those who were thinking of the Party's prospects (as opposed to the dinner party prospects) that all those other candidates who had been unwilling to stand the first time might stop her on the second ballot and then, even if she had a simple majority on the third ballot, deny her victory through the operation of second preference. Such a gerrymandered sort of result would produce a dangerous divide between the Party at Westminster and that in the country where opinion had now definitely firmed up in Mrs Thatcher's favour. There was thus, as the *Daily Telegraph* reported, a growing feeling that it would be better for the Party and the country to get the whole thing over by seeing that on the second ballot the lady won outright.

To counter this feeling the Whitelaw supporters were arguing that Mrs Thatcher's appeal was too narrowly southern, whereas their man could restore the Conservative fortunes among the workers in the north. Yet, as Mr John O'Sullivan pointed out in a witty sketch in the *Daily Telegraph*, this idea was rather curious. For Mr Whitelaw, who was a regular old Wykehamist toff, and a landowner to boot, while he might pass as a northerner in Westminster, would be a southerner in Leeds. Besides, the concept of the northerners as impoverished clog-wearing proletarians was decidedly misleading. The suburban belt in Cheshire was as ritzy as anything Surrey could offer. Why should it be assumed that the people of the north would resent the rise to power of a girl from a Lincolnshire grammar school? Why assume that the northerners, with their great industrial tradition, would decry a leader with a robust, unapologetic belief in free enterprise?

In view of recent events, it was indeed a quaint notion that under Mrs Thatcher the Tory Party would only appeal to the suburban south-east. For the narrowing of the bases of Conservative support occurred under the later Heath policy with which her main rivals were intending to continue, *not* under the 1970 policy on which the Conservatives had won and to which she was proposing to return. As Lord Coleraine, a former Minister and the son of a former Prime Minister (Bonar Law) pointed out in a timely letter to the *Daily Telegraph* on 7 February, the fatal weakening of the Conservative Party arose from the attempt to be all things to all men. What was needed to appeal to the floating voters was the ability to inspire them with a sense of conviction, and Mrs Thatcher alone among the candidates for Leader, he contended, had that gift. He aptly quoted the opinion of an earlier Prime Minister, Lord Salisbury, on middle-of-the-road Conservatism, that the Party would lose more by alarming its normal supporters than it would ever gain by bidding for the gratitude of those who were not. 'You may say that they cannot vote against you, but they won't vote for you, and they won't work for you, and you'll find it out at the polls.'

On the Friday the Government released details of its new concessions on Capital Transfer Tax, aimed particularly at reducing the impact on small businesses and farms. Under it, lifetime gifts would be charged at half the rate charged if the assets were transferred at death. This was something of a success for Mrs Thatcher who had led the assault on the original proposals and she said, 'This is a major relief, and we are grateful for it. It will be a very much less severe tax as a result.'

On the Saturday both Mrs Thatcher and Mr Whitelaw were billed to speak at the Young Conservatives' Annual Conference at Eastbourne. Mr Whitelaw must have been heartened by *The Times* leader that morning, which came down in his favour even if the main argument it used was rather bizarre. Mr Whitelaw, it urged, was a comfortable man from whom the public would accept the harsh measures that would be needed. 'But the future of the Conservative Party could hang on an even simpler personal matter; Mr Heath and Mr Whitelaw like each other, and Mr Heath and Mrs Thatcher do not. A successful relationship between a new leader and an old can only be built where there is some affection and regard on both sides.' The logic of this was weird to say the least. For a start, a man who was so outstandingly 'comfortable' would presumably be ill disposed to the idea of taking harsh measures at all, whatever the situation might demand. More likely he would choose the most immediately comfortable course of action and march away from the sound of gunfire. Again, having rejected Mr Heath and what he stood for, what possible reason would the Party have for effectively giving the rejected leader the power to nominate his successor? Besides, where did the idea come from that a Party can only be run on the basis of a successful working relationship between the new Leader and the one who has just had the boot? If so the chances of changing course would be poor indeed. Perhaps the confusion arose from an editorial feeling of guilt in having gone too far in recommending Mr Heath's dismissal in the first ballot, a guilt for which it was now trying desperately to compensate.

At first glance the omens at Eastbourne were inauspicious. Mr Clive Landa, the Young Conservative Chairman, had been an ardent Heath supporter (indeed his wife Frances was wearing black to symbolise her mourning for the departed leader) and, by the same token, he could be assumed to be a Whitelaw supporter too. Moreover, the Young Conservatives had tended in the past to veer to the left. Yet in practice it proved to be Mrs Thatcher's day. Mr Whitelaw arrived first in a crumpled grey suit and took questions from the audience on the rather dull subjects of devolution and the Party organisation. He made little use of the occasion to expound his political philosophy and the applause was muted. Mrs Thatcher, by contrast, arrived fresh and smiling in a bright turquoise dress and no hat. Her role was to reply to an economic affairs debate, which she did in spirited fashion, beginning with a merry quip about the leadership contest. 'By this stage of the week', she said, 'I'm beginning to think "that was the week that was" but it looks like next week will be another one.' She also said 'If Willie can be photographed scouring pots and pans, who knows, I may be photographed on the golf course.' (A reference to a rather absurd press picture of Willie in the kitchen and the fact that he is an outstanding golfer and captain of the Royal and Ancient). She then slightly bent the rules and proceeded to give her five-minute political credo. 'Our challenge is to create the kind

[128]

of economic background which enables private initiative and private enterprise to flourish for the benefit of the consumer, the employee, the pensioner, and society as a whole . . . the person who is prepared to work hardest should get the greatest rewards and keep them after tax.' (Applause.) 'We should back the workers and not the shirkers.' (Applause.) 'It is not only permissible but praiseworthy to want to benefit your own family by your own efforts.' (Much applause.) 'Liberty must never be confused with licence and you cannot have liberty without a just law impartially administered.' (Applause.) 'You would not have political liberty for long if all power and property went to the State.' (Applause.) 'Those who prosper themselves have a duty and responsibility to care for others.' This, according to the breezy account of the meeting by the *Observer*'s correspondent, Robert Chesshyre, produced a sixty-seven second count of applause and the first kiss of the day from the Chairman. She then went along the seafront with Willie and, to show there was no hard feeling and to the delight of the photographers, was kissed by him too. It was not for the first time it seems. 'I have kissed her often before' but not 'on a pavement outside a hotel in Eastbourne.'

The Eastbourne Conference was palpably, and against expectation, a big boost for Mrs Thatcher. Yet, the bookmakers were still, at this time, putting Mr Whitelaw in the lead. William Hill's were quoting Whitelaw 13-8 on and Thatcher 7-4 against, with the other contenders nowhere. Some of the press were suggesting that Mr Prior was about to overtake Mr Whitelaw as the 'middle-of-the-road' candidate. The following day there were reports that soundings in the constituencies showed two to one in favour of Mrs Thatcher. This was more significant than the previous support for Mr Heath, which could be to some extent written off as the instinctive loyalty for the leader. In the Thatcher case support was more likely to reflect a free choice between alternatives.

Of course it was within the Parliamentary Party that the

issue was to be decided, and there Mr Whitelaw was undoubtedly suffering from the earlier sapping and mining of all possible rivals by the Heath lobby. They had done their work too well and had little time to reverse it. Insidiously they had spread the word that Mr Whitelaw was not up to the job, that he was not bright enough. In fact this was unjust. Mr Whitelaw is rather shrewd, but his shrewdness is more about people than about issues. He is strong on the human qualities, he has a remarkable flair for parliamentary tactics, but his very affability had counted against his developing the lethal debating skill in which Mrs Thatcher was now emerging supreme.

Mr Airey Neave's low-profile approach to the election again appears to have been well judged. In accordance with this policy, Mrs Thatcher refused to take part in the 'Panorama' programme meant to include all five contestants: she concentrated instead on meetings with potential supporters among MPs. The official explanation was that the format of the programme did not suit her, but the real worry was that the programme, whether intentionally or not, might be loaded against her, and no amount of apology after the event could undo the harm of a lost election.

The Peers were two to one in favour of Mr Whitelaw, but the bookies had at last got round to quoting odds on Mrs Thatcher, perhaps influenced by the *Daily Mail's* poll of Tory MPs the previous day which put her on top. Even so, nothing was certain. Who could say but that some last-minute gust of sentiment might not start a stampede for Whitelaw or Prior or Peyton or Howe? Or what if Mrs Thatcher were stopped now and the others ganged up against her?

This time there were no abstainers among the 276 Conservative members, though (strangely for people who must be voting experts) there were two spoiled papers. Mr Patrick Wall, the member for Haltemprice, actually cut short a visit to South Africa and flew back to London for the special purpose

[132]

of recording his vote. The result could scarcely have been more decisive. It was:

Mrs Margaret Thatcher	146
Mr William Whitelaw	79
Sir Geoffrey Howe	19
Mr James Prior	19
Mr John Peyton	11

Mrs Thatcher was radiant with her success. As she went to a Press Conference in a room of Westminster Hall she was warmly cheered and congratulated by members of the National Association of Widows who had just left their meeting. In the Press Conference her emphasis was all on the need for conciliation and Party teamwork. Asked about changes, she said that she was asking the present Shadow Cabinet to carry on for the time being, but Mr Whitelaw would certainly stay in her Shadow Cabinet. Asked if she was going to make more openings for women, she said the first thing was to get more women into Parliament 'and then we shall be less conspicuous'. It was certainly a great day for the women and in this respect party affiliations made no difference. Indeed, from her earliest days in the House, Mrs Thatcher had found a touching camaraderie among the members of her sex. The joy of Mrs Renée Short was almost unconfined. 'There is no doubt', she said 'that Mrs Thatcher is a remarkably able woman, but she has probably had to fight harder to gain the leadership than any man.' That was certainly true. Mr Whitelaw sent his congratulations and wishes for future success. The all-male Carlton Club in St James's (subscription £100 a year), traditionally the London Club of the Conservative Leader, offered her honorary membership. There was enormous interest and curiosity all over the world and especially on the European Continent. Fancy the British Conservatives making a woman their Leader! Whatever next? In Paris Mme Giroud, Secretary of State for Women's Affairs, said Mrs Thatcher's election was a 'spectacular and very amusing success'.

Amusing? Yes, she said, because the men would panic!

Of course there were celebrations galore and a family celebration with champagne. Yet, Mrs Thatcher found time to drop in to the Commons Standing Committee on the Finance Bill, where she had worked and fought so hard, where she had her triumphs and had won the respect of friend and foe alike. There she was cheered by Labour as well as Conservative MPs, and Mr Joel Barnett, Labour's Chief Secretary of the Treasury, and from all accounts one of the nicest of men, offered his congratulations too. 'We hope you enjoy the best of health', he said. 'If you go on looking as attractive as you do tonight it will be very beneficial.' So even among the sophists, calculators and economists of the Treasury Front Bench, who said that the age of chivalry was dead?

12

HONEYMOON
PERIOD

On Wednesday, the day after the second ballot, Mrs
Thatcher took her seat as Opposition Leader in the House of
Commons, where she was flanked on either side by her former
rivals, Messrs Whitelaw, Prior, Peyton and Sir Geoffrey Howe.
She made a brief foray on the subject of the royal finances. Mr
Harold Wilson, who was on unusually good form, then
launched into a well prepared and rather funny speech. He
wished Mrs Thatcher happiness, referred to her three
predecessors, whom he had seen off, and then mentioned the
discussions which were customary between the Party Leaders.
'I look forward', he said, 'to meetings behind the Speaker's
chair, and to the informality and intimacy they afford.' For
some reason, perhaps the accumulated strain of the preceding
weeks, Mrs Thatcher did not even respond with a smile, but she
did rise and thanked Mr Wilson for his kindness.

Naturally there was now great speculation as to what the
new Leader would do about her Shadow Cabinet. Her first move
was to call on Mr Heath and offer him a place in it, which,
however, he refused. Her second move was to offer Mr
Whitelaw, who had been her main rival for the leadership, the

post of Deputy Leader of the Opposition which he accepted. Yet these conciliatory gestures only whetted the appetites of the commentators, and produced an avalanche of advice. Some of it was rather sour, especially that from quarters like *The Economist* and the *Observer*, which had been consistently hostile to her and had minimised her chances of winning. The panjandrums of the lobby now almost united in suggesting that she should abandon her right-wing supporters, and what one called her primitive Goldwater-like instincts, and opt for the middle way in which her predecessor was standing when he got run over in February 1974. If Mrs Thatcher took any notice of all this unctuous advice then there is no evidence of it; as usual she made up her own mind. On the Monday the main Shadow Cabinet changes were announced. She had dropped six members of the Heath team, namely Mr Robert Carr (Treasury) and Mr Peter Walker (Defence), Mr Geoffrey Rippon (Foreign and Commonwealth), Mr Paul Channon (Environment), Mr Nicholas Scott (Housing), and Mr Peter Thomas (Wales). The main replacements were Mr Reginald Maudling (Foreign Affairs), Sir Keith Joseph (number three in the Shadow Cabinet with a roving brief on policy and research), Sir Geoffrey Howe (Treasury), Mr Ian Gilmour (Home Office), Mr Timothy Raison (Environment), Mr George Younger (Defence), Mr Airey Neave (Northern Ireland, while remaining in charge of Mrs Thatcher's private office) and Mrs Sally Oppenheim (Consumer Affairs). The choice of Mr Maudling (the Poulson case, from which he was totally exonerated of blame, being over) struck most commentators as imaginative. The inclusion of Sir Geoffrey Howe and Mr Ian Gilmour in senior positions showed that Mrs Thatcher had decided to forget the leadership struggle and set about rebuilding Party unity.

If anything was needed to bring home to Mrs Thatcher that she was now one of the Western World's top people, it was the arrival, just before the announcement of these changes, of Dr

Kissinger, who gave her breakfast. 'Just keep talking,' said Dr Kissinger as they posed for photographers. 'What does your husband do?' 'Oh, he's in oil,' she said. The Doctor, who had just come from Saudi Arabia, apparently looked impressed. Then they went and had a traditional English breakfast. It seems that Dr Kissinger had enquired as to what Tory ladies like, with the result that, in addition to bacon and eggs, she was offered muffins.

As if this was not enough public exposure for one week, Mrs Thatcher next day went on Jimmy Young's lunch-time programme on Radio 2. There she said that her day as Tory 'butcher' (when she wielded the axe on her colleagues) was 'horrid', revealed that she had not worn a twin-set for ten years, and claimed she was the right age to be Leader—'I'm nudging fifty, I'm no chicken.'

Mrs Thatcher was still only, formally speaking, Leader of the Conservative Party in the House of Commons: she had yet to be formally proclaimed Leader of the Party in the country. This was done at a gathering representing all sections of the Party, at the Europa Hotel in Mayfair. Tributes were paid, sincerely enough, to Mr Heath the former Leader, who, however, was on holiday in Spain. Then Lord Hailsham proposed that Mrs Thatcher be adopted Leader, Mr Whitelaw seconded the motion, followed by representatives of the National Union etc., and she was adopted *nemine contradicente* to tumultuous applause. Mrs Thatcher then appeared, looking radiant in a smart turquoise outfit, and gave a rousing speech. She said that what people wanted was a forthright style of leadership, with more emphasis on principle, and she pledged herself to give them just that, with all her strength, loyalty and determination. It was a happy gathering, and all the more so because the Gallup Poll in the *Daily Telegraph* brought news of a huge 18½ per cent swing to the Conservatives, giving them a 4 per cent lead. The poll also indicated that the mass of voters, Labour as well as Conservative, thought Mrs Thatcher would make a good

Leader.

This poll was of course national. But what about those doubts voiced earlier that Mrs Thatcher's appeal was nevertheless confined to the home counties? Her visit to Scotland the day after (necessary because the Scottish Conservatives are a separate body from those in England and Wales) dispelled these anxieties. In both Glasgow and Edinburgh people turned out in their thousands. She made a stirring attack on Socialism and bureaucracy, skilfully harped on choice in education—a very Scottish concern—made no concessions to Scottish nationalism, and took them all by storm. Alighting from the train the next day at 5.32 a.m., a press photographer was waiting, but, even at that time, unruffled and clutching a bouquet of flowers, she was still 'looking like a new pin'.

The second tier of Shadow Cabinet appointments, announced on February 25, was like the first in its attempt to keep a balance between the two wings of the Party and was otherwise only notable for putting the accent on youth. More newsworthy were the new appointments at Conservative Central Office. Under these Lord Thorneycroft became the Party Chairman, Mr Angus Maude Deputy Chairman—both of them to be members of the Shadow Cabinet. Both men had well deserved reputations for independence of mind, for both had in the past suffered loss of office because they could not agree with their leader. Mr Thorneycroft, as he then was, along with Mr Nigel Birch and Mr Enoch Powell, had resigned from the Macmillan Government in protest against excessive deficit spending, and was thus one of the first martyrs of the monetarist cause. Mr Maude had lost his seat in Mr Heath's Shadow Cabinet after writing an article criticising the leadership in January 1966. That Mrs Thatcher was not looking for yes-men or people who were too junior to contradict her was evident, both from these appointments and from the earlier one of Mr Airey Neave in charge of her personal office.

For Mr Neave, a war hero and an industrialist, and a Member of Parliament at an age when he no longer hungered for political advancement, had enough seniority, personal standing and detachment to tell her exactly what he thought.

There were now many speaking engagements as Party Leader which Mrs Thatcher had to take over at short notice from Mr Heath, while she tried her best to maintain commitments which she already had. One of the latter was at Beaminster in Dorset, where she had promised to speak for Mr Jim Spicer, a new MP of the February 1974 vintage. Although Beaminster is a small place, about 2,000 people turned up. She referred to the recent comment on her by Mr David Wood, Political Editor of *The Times* (and, incidentally, another product of her home town, for he started his career in the *Grantham Journal*) who had said that, 'The art of political survival is to deal with the facts as they are and not to dream dreams.' She was a practical politician, she said, but how depressing not to dream dreams. 'That is the fate of the bureaucrats, not the inspiration of statesmen . . . . Did not Disraeli dream dreams? Nor Churchill? . . . We will deal with the facts as they are all right. But we will make some dreams come true as well.' She departed from the text of her prepared speech to attack the Capital Transfer Tax, which she was at this time busily opposing in the House, and she warned this more than usually rural gathering of the danger that the tax presented to farming and forestry, not to mention small businesses, and argued that it would, if left alone, adversely change the face of Britain within a generation.

Her next appearance, a strictly Party one this time, was before 300 Conservative Trade Unionists at their annual conference. She urged them, as representing the reasonable, moderate majority, to action against the determined fanatical minority groups who were manipulating events in the interest of extreme political cults. This not entirely original sentiment was delivered with enthusiasm and received with an ovation. It was heartening that she retained her oratorical bounce when there was so much more to do. At her office there were 18,000 well-wishers' letters to be answered, and an avalanche of requests from the media for interviews, articles and broadcasts, not only in Britain, but all over the world, where interest in the first British woman to lead a political party was intense.

Yet euphoria in politics never endures: the harsh imperatives of power have a habit of appearing, spectre-like, when festivities are at their height, and the trouble had now focused on Central Office. There Lord Thorneycroft, after taking a good look at the organisational set-up and finding it wanting, suddenly dismissed the Director General, Mr Michael Wolff. The original appointment a year earlier of Mr Wolff, who had long been 'personal adviser' (a euphemism for 'speech writer') to Mr Heath, had been almost as dramatic as his departure. For he had been suddenly plonked on top of all the existing already topheavy top brass and given overall responsibility. His job as such was now abolished, and its administrative side put in the hands of Mr William Clarke, MP for Croydon South, who, unlike Mr Wolff at his appointment, had already had considerable experience of the Party's inner workings as one of the Party Treasurers.

The dismissal aroused considerable ire among former Heath supporters. Mr Barney Hayhoe pronounced it absurd, and Mr James Prior was so put out that he missed voting on the Finance Bill in the House of Commons. *The Times*, on the day that Mrs Thatcher was due to talk to the 1922 Committee, thundered from the leader page the strangely intemperate comment that it was 'the act of a downright fool'. It portrayed Mr Wolff as a great young reforming administrator being fired by a lot of fuddy-duddies, making an unworthy and inaccurate attack on Mr Clarke as a person of narrow right-wing views. Mr Rees Mogg, the *Times* Editor, is loyal to friends, of whom Mr Wolff is fortunate to rank as one.

It was no doubt a pity that Mr Wolff should have had to suffer these traumas—he is an estimable, good natured man and a competent journalist, but it is no reflection on his abilities to say that the qualification which was most important in fitting him for the post originally was his ardent attachment to Mr Heath and his policies. Arguably this was more of a disqualification than a recommendation for Mr Heath's successor, who had arrived on a wave of discontent with Mr Heath and his policies. As Mr Alan Watkins pithily put it in the *New Statesman*, 'those that live by patronage shall surely perish by patronage, but Mr Wolff will, I am sure, quickly find another job.' Lord Lambton later commented in the *Evening Standard* that one of Mr Heath's major faults was that he could not communicate, and the fact that Mr Wolff wrote many of his speeches 'is surely sufficient reason for his dismissal', but this was unjust. Mr Wolff wrote what he was instructed to write. As many who devilled for Mr Heath will confirm, he was much given to crossing out any striking phrases in any copy prepared for him and substituting a cliché. Lord Lambton was more pertinent, however, in his reflection that, 'It is said that Mr Wolff was improving Central Office, but Mr Heath had been leader of the Party for ten years with Mr Wolff as his closest assistant, so Central Office is what they made it, and few can criticise Mrs Thatcher's determination to improve its efficiency.'

Mrs Thatcher plainly had no intention of yielding to factional pressures over the most important professional appointment in her gift: and, as ever, she was busy. There was her first Party Political Broadcast which went out on the same night as the Wolff dismissal was announced. Her theme was the threat of a Labour Party dominated by the left wing due to an unholy combination of 'Bigot Benn, Foolish Foot and Wily Wilson'. Such alliteration is, of course, part of the tricks of the orator's trade and it was nice to have a leader again with some relish for words. The response was generally favourable. Jean Rook in the *Daily Mail* thought that Mrs Thatcher was 'a little too lovely' in her cream linen safari suit, and flanked by pot plants (though she would vote for her just the same), but James Murray, the *Express* TV critic pronounced her 'a trouper'. Like many others he particularly warmed to her parting shot: 'To yesterday's men Tomorrow's Woman says Hello.' He also wondered whether there was anything significant in the fact that she arrived in the studio clutching a book entitled *Invective & Abuse*.

Back in the House of Commons there was a debate on the proposed referendum on whether Britain should stay in Europe. Mr Callaghan, the Foreign Secretary, had brought back 'renegotiated' terms from Brussels, and the Government had issued a White Paper recommending acceptance. The whole renegotiation caper was indeed a charade, and amounted to little more than forcing into an artificial package a number of issues on which Britain would normally have been making representation in Brussels in the ordinary course of Community business. The only purpose of the referendum had been to provide a formula for overcoming Labour's internal split over Europe. What were the Conservatives to do in the debate? The decision was taken to vote against the referendum, while preparing to propagate the European idea, spearheaded by a group of Conservative MPs under Mr Eldon Griffiths, if the referendum took place. The debate had a special importance for Mrs Thatcher, because it was the occasion of her maiden speech as Tory Party Leader. This time she took as her punchbag Mr Short, her old opponent on Education, and now Leader of the House, and proceeded politely, but efficiently, and to the delight of her back-benchers, to lay into him. She questioned the status of the referendum. What size poll and what majority added up to 'full hearted consent'? What was the use of saying that Parliament retained a theoretical sovereignty, if you had to add in the next breath, as Mr Short did, that MPs could not be expected to go against the wishes of the people? 'It's just a tactical device to get over a split in their own Party', Mrs Thatcher said in conclusion. 'The people must make a decision. Parliament must make a decision, but the Government is incapable of making a decision.' Gone was the discipline of resignation, of accountability. 'Pass the buck to the people'—that was the new doctrine.

Mrs Thatcher showed her increasingly nimble footwork in this speech. She quoted Dicey (the constitutional lawyer) in her support and Mr Michael Stewart, former Labour Foreign Secretary and writer of a book on political theory, caused loud laughter by pointing out that Dicey also thought it against nature for women to help elect MPs. To this Mrs Thatcher replied, unabashed, 'Women get on all right in the Tory Party.'

It was a good parliamentary performance, and gave heart to the Tory back-benches, except those occupied by fervent anti-marketeers. It was not an easy case the Conservatives were putting—it too easily looked like a disbelief in the principle of popular consent. Also, most people seemed to think that Labour had done some good for the country by producing more favourable revised terms. At least, that was the message of the public opinion polls. For while the Gallup Poll, for which the research was done at this time, (though the results were published a week later) showed Labour back in the lead by 2 per cent, the Harris Poll, published a week earlier, and for which interviewing had taken place just after Mrs Thatcher's election, had shown the Tories leading by 8 per cent. As it happened, a couple of days after the debate Mr Trudeau, the Canadian Prime Minister, came to London on one stage of his tour of Common Market capitals. He spoke of the desirability of a contractual link between his country and the EEC, came and talked to Mr Wilson and Mr Callaghan, and before going on to receive the honorary freedom of the City stopped for half an hour's talk with Mrs Thatcher. When photographers asked them to move closer Mrs Thatcher said, 'Oh, you are saucy!'

It had been suggested in the past that a few saucy things were going to be said, especially by the Young Conservatives, about the Shadow Cabinet and Central Office changes at the

Conservative Party's Central Council, which was already meeting at Harrogate. The Central Council is a sort of Party Conference in miniature, though with 800 delegates it is not as miniature as all that. As it turned out, there was little complaint. The theme of the speakers from the floor boiled down to 'Get the state off our backs', which was music to Mrs Thatcher's ears and was in harmony with her own message when she went up and spoke on the last day. She expressed 'a profound belief—indeed a fervent faith—in the virtues of self-reliance and independence. On these is founded the whole case for the free society, and for the assertion that human progress is best achieved by offering the freest possible scope for the development of individual talents, qualified only by a respect for the qualities and the freedom of others.'

In Britain, she continued, freedom was being eroded. 'Self reliance is sneered at as an absurd suburban pretension.' Thrift was equated with greed, honourable ambition frustrated, and the small business strangled by taxes, while people were encouraged to flout the law. This latter theme she expanded at the Tory Local Government Conference at Southport, where she attacked the Labour Government for indemnifying the councillors at Clay Cross, apparently on the principle that law-breakers should not suffer 'provided they break the law in the Labour interest'.

These sentiments were well received, but some commentators criticised them as generalities. It was a refreshing change, though, after the surfeit of particularities served up under her predecessor. Of course, for a balanced diet it is necessary to have some of both. Yet at this stage the Conservatives' urgent need was not for a plethora of policy specifics but rather the basis upon which to decide, in the broadest terms, the nature of the country's afflictions, and what the aims and priorities of Government should be. For diagnosis must necessarily precede prescription and disaster will come to the politician, no less than to the surgeon, who has only a hazy idea of what ails the patient, but is determined to operate at all costs. The cardinal ills of our society are, indeed, what Mrs Thatcher chose to highlight in this speech—anarchy's growth and freedom's decay. Mrs Thatcher finished her speech with a pledge to fight these menacing trends. It remains to be considered what in future this is likely to involve.

13

FIRST
WOMAN
PRIME MINISTER

When Mrs Thatcher was Minister of Education she rather surprised some of her civil servants in the middle of a meeting by looking at her watch and saying, 'I've just time to pop down to the grocer's on the corner to buy some bacon for Denis.' When it was suggested that a secretary might go, she said, 'No. I know just the cut he likes.' It is one of her strengths that she has retained her links with normal every-day life. The pictures of her collecting the milk which appeared during the leadership contest were not contrived, for she really does do many of the household chores herself and always did, even when she was a Senior Minister. She has, however, only managed to combine a successful political career with raising a family and keeping two homes through considerable self-discipline, remarkable energy and intelligent organisation. She makes lists of things to be done and ticks them off as she does them—what management consultants grandly call 'linear programming'. She also is fortunate in needing little sleep—she rarely gets to bed before 1.30 a.m. and gets up around seven to make early morning tea and a hearty breakfast for the family. Until recently she did the shopping and took her dirty washing to the launderette. She really likes cooking and, when she has time, decorating the home. She eats her meals quickly, drinks alcohol sparingly and does not smoke at all—in 1974 she was nominated 'Non-smoker of the Year'. She drives well and has never been summonsed for an offence, not even for parking. Mrs Thatcher has sometimes been too busy to take an annual holiday, but in the past the family used to go skiing, though in recent years she has taken the view that the danger of an accident counts it out and now they go to the Isle of Wight. In her spare time she looks at television, reads detective novels, plays the piano, and goes a good deal to opera at Glyndebourne and Covent Garden. She reads *The Times, Daily Mail* and *Daily Telegraph*.

The years have dealt kindly with Mrs Thatcher and her figure has actually become slimmer. She is always well turned out, though she buys her clothes off the peg and spends little time doing so. Her favourites are dresses with matching jackets and patterned skirts. She frequently wears a string of pearls which her husband gave her for her birthday and which were often picked on by unfriendly critics who would find her twin set and pearls somehow symbolic of upper-class snobbery, though, as she told Jimmy Young when she appeared on his show, she had not worn a twin set for ten years. She wears a gold bracelet containing multi-coloured stones (also a birthday present from Denis) all the time since she was lucky enough to be wearing it when her house was burgled during the February 1974 Election. She goes regularly to have her hair done at Chalmer's in Mayfair, which, according to Ann Kent in the *Daily Mail,* is, despite its address, 'as middle-class as the voters Mrs Thatcher hopes to woo back the Tory cause'.

It is not only normalcy that gives stability to her active, organised life, but—and how normal is this?—a happy married life. It is perhaps lucky that Denis Thatcher, who is due to retire before this book is published, has also been a very busy man. The family paint factory in Dartford, of which he was managing director when he met his wife to be, was later taken over by Castrol, which was itself taken over by Burmah Oil. He went with his firm and finished his career as Burmah Oil's Financial Planning Director. He is an able, very hard-working, straightforward man, who is genuinely proud of his wife's achievements. He is a modest golfer and has the even more strenuous hobby of refereeing rugby matches. Of the twins, the son Mark went to Harrow, where he was Captain of Racquets, but though he was entered for Oxford he decided to go straight into chartered accountancy in which he is now qualified. He is an extrovert, a games-playing type who does some motor-racing, and was a great support to his mother in the hectic days of the leadership election which he rather enjoyed. His sister Carol liked the family publicity much less, partly because she was taking her law examinations at the time—one reporter even called her up in the middle of an examination paper! She has therefore chosen to work in the provinces in order to avoid the limelight. She is an articled clerk with a legal firm in Chichester where her employers consider her very clever. The children had to put up with a certain amount of stick from their fellows in the days when their mother was Minister for Education, especially as she was so unpopular with students, but they seem to have survived very well.

Some unfriendly critics have been apt to fasten on to the fact that Mrs Thatcher was not much given to returning home to Grantham after leaving Oxford and starting her career, and this is made the basis for suggesting that she was heartlessly ambitious, abandoning the old folks at home. In fact all the evidence is that she was deeply attached to her father (while her sister was closer to her mother), for whom indeed no sacrifice was too great to see that she (and her sister too) got every chance in life; but she was also a little in awe of him. She has remained throughout on intimate terms with her sister, Muriel, whom she incidentally introduced to her farmer husband in 1948. She has also kept her friendships in good repair with those few intimates of school and college days, though most of

[148]

Study of the victor, 1975

Just for the record – with Jimmy Young, 1975

Three for Europe – with the President and Secretary General of
the European Parliament, 1975

Leading Lady, 1975

Off the cuff with Reagan, 1975

Answers for well-wishers, 1975

'Looking like a new pin', 1975

With Pierre Trudeau, 1975

At the Elysée – with President Giscard d'Estaing, 1975

'My husband's in oil', 1975

United for Europe, 1975

Ideal Home, 1975

them are living rather a long distance from London. She is kind in a very practical way. One childhood friend she told years ago (and has often been taken up on it) never to go wasting money on hotels when she came to London, but to come and stay at the Thatcher home in Chelsea. She is not a great one for going to stay with people herself; as she is so busy in the week she likes to be at home and relax with her own family at weekends. She tends to make friends, like many other people, among those with whom she is working and who are mentally on net with her, such as Mr Norman St John Stevas at the Education Ministry, or Mr Airey Neave whom oddly enough she met when she was candidate at Dartford and was a pupil in the same chambers as him when she went into law.

On this bright, elegant, nice, home-loving lady now falls one of the most exciting yet formidable tasks that a Conservative Leader has ever in peace times been set. The immediate problem for the Conservatives is the electoral one. This is to win back the old supporters, especially among the working class and in the North, who abandoned them in the two elections of 1974, and to redress the grievances of their faithful but disgruntled supporters, like the people on fixed incomes. The longer-term problem is to formulate a policy which will put the country back on its feet.

From an electoral point of view, as we have seen, and contrary to the frantic warnings of her detractors in the leadership contest, Mrs Thatcher is turning out to be a palpable asset and probably one of enduring value. For her appeal is only in part due to her novelty as the first woman leader, at least if her eager reception in Glasgow at the end of February and the subsequent victories in the urban elections are anything to judge by. It is also because this particular female has considerable demagogic qualities. Her sense of the language of oratory is much superior to that of most of her political contemporaries. This is probably not due to her legal training because the political speeches of barristers can be dreadfully prolix (because professionally they tend to be paid according to active agent for the disintegration of the English tongue). As must be clear after reading this far, Mrs Thatcher is unusual three times on every Sunday (as opposed to the New English Bible, the first instalment of which was dubbed by T.S. Eliot an active agent for the disintegration of the English tongue). As must be clear after reading this far, Mrs Thatcher is unusual in her political generation for the trouble she has consistently taken over her public utterances and in the process she has developed a personal style which is pungent, forceful and direct. Undoubtedly, to bring Flaubert's dictum up to date for the era of Women's Lib, 'Style is the woman'. It is a style which we may note *en passant* owes nothing to PR men, because Mrs Thatcher has been in the habit of writing her speeches herself.

Still, style and presentation are one thing, the message under the gift wrapping another. Have those who see Mrs Thatcher as the epitome of the South East suburban housewife got a point? Do her natural sympathies tally with those of the working class in the North for instance? According to Mr Max Taylor (*Crossbow,* April 1975), who was twice a Tory candidate for Hull West and who conducted a thorough survey canvass of his working-class constituency, the answer is 'Yes'. His survey canvass, in which people were simply asked what issues they thought were important, or what they wanted to get done, resulted in the following list:

Dislike of the economic and social power of the Unions.
Concern with rising prices.
Dislike of high taxation.
Dislike of shirkers on Social Security.
Concern for law, order and discipline.
Fear of further immigration.
A keen sense of patriotism—what must we do to put the
country right?

One has only to look down this list to see that Mrs Thatcher scores heavily compared, for instance, to Mr Heath or those who competed with her on the second ballot. It was interesting that, of the articles contributed to the *Daily Telegraph* by the leadership contenders, only Mrs Thatcher and her ally Sir Keith Joseph said that the defeat of inflation must have overriding priority compared with other objectives—full employment for instance. On union power (referring to the same article) she was noticeably lukewarm about the rather vague Heath ideas of national unity achieved through power-sharing with the Unions (and the CBI). For it is a great mistake to see the Heath policy as one of 'getting tough with the Unions'. Certainly it was a policy which, in its tactics, brought confrontation with the unions, but the formula for settlement and peace thereafter amounted to a partial surrender to the unions in the sense that it in effect offered to take them into partnership in governing the country. The Thatcher/Joseph idea of running the economy with greater monetary restraint and economy in public spending is far more likely to keep the unions under restraint than the earlier Tory Government's policy of pump priming or lighting a fire under the economic kettle in order to produce expansion and full employment while holding the incomes policy lid on.

As for Mrs Thatcher's dislike of high taxation, that is proverbial, while she is one of the few leading Tories who will unblushingly talk about shirkers. She identifies with the average working-class folk as opposed to the Hampstead set in her contempt for spongers and has no upper-class guilt feelings to stop her saying so. Her desire for stern measures against law-breakers is vehement, and she has never suffered from any inhibitions about mouthing such 'reactionary' sentiments as that the victim deserves our sympathies more than the criminal. Her experience with students in their worst period of unrest (though this never threw her or undermined her tolerance, and she said at the time there could be no question of withdrawing students' grants for rebelliousness) gave her an unusual awareness of one aspect of the problem of violence and the threat of subversion of traditional institutions. With two children of her own going through higher education she also had a direct insight into the parents' point of view, in which again she was pretty typical, being indulgent without being permissive.

As far as the record goes, Mrs Thatcher seems to have made no significant pronouncement one way or the other on immigration. Her interest in foreign affairs has not been marked either, but that is perhaps no bad thing. Those, especially of the previous generation to her, who have taken a special interest in foreign affairs, have been a bit too lofty in their outlook. Indeed it is our leaders' excessive pretensions supported on a weakening economic base which have helped to accelerate Britain's decline ever since the Second World War. Rather less high-mindedness and more simple patriotism, less of the world moral leadership nonsense and more low profile *realpolitik* seems now to be what is required—for example, sorting out our *own* inflation and reducing our *own* external debts rather than sponsoring grandiose international plans for recycling Arab dollars!

So, on the criteria enumerated above, Mrs Thatcher looks remarkably well qualified to restore her Party's fortunes among what may, for brevity's sake, be called the Northern Working Class. She has the style and attitudes to make her an effective populist. But what about the grievances of the traditional Conservative supporter, the one who abstained or defected to the Liberals on occasions like the Orpington or Sutton by-elections, such as the retired with a fixed, or more or less fixed income, the suburban clerk or professional worker who has higher fares, higher rates and higher mortgage interest to pay, but is left behind in the wages race, and the parent whose only chance of giving his children a good education is through the local grammar school, especially as the direct grant schools disappear, and the small shopkeeper whose receipts do not keep pace with rising costs and is squeezed still further by price control? For such the Thatcher message is reassuring, too reassuring some might say, thinking that it smacks too much of Poujadism. Yet what Mrs Thatcher and her policy maker, Sir Keith Joseph, in general stand for on this matter is not sectional protectionism but justice, the justice of being protected against being deprived of legitimate expectations. This is the wider context of what the Thatcher package on mortgages and rates was trying to do. Call it 'indexation', call it an interim exercise to alleviate the distributive injustice of inflation, and much of the criticism would disappear. Yet, on the other side of the coin of indexation, there must be a government determined to staunch the monetary source of inflation or else the coin is a dud. From that point of view, too, the Thatcher/Joseph combination is credible in its bid for the right to make these national decisions in a way that its rivals from whatever party are not.

Mrs Thatcher gives confidence in the further sense that she talks without apology about middle-class values of thrift and hard work, but she avoids the trap of sectionalism in pointing out, rightly, that those values are not confined to one class even if there are historical class associations—the puritan ethic of the bourgeoisie—which cling to them.

Reviewing Mrs Thatcher's victory just after the event, Mr David Watt of the *Financial Times* saw her as a true revolutionary. The Tory Party, he said, had historically evolved from being an aristocratic Party with some middle-class additions, to being a middle-class Party with some working-class additions at one end and some landowning relics at the other. In the course of that evolution the middle class got taught aristocratic (and also pietist) values in Arnold-style public schools. This process created a British middle class quite unlike that on the Continent, bland, tolerant, high-minded. The 'dominant ethic' of the Tory Party in this country, so Mr Watt argues, has been that of Oxbridge, the armed services and the professions, that is, associated with the Empire, bureaucracy and the tradition of paternalism. Their attitude of effortless superiority was maintained long past the point where both the Empire and the social and economic foundations of their power as a governing class had disappeared. The upper-middle-class Tories were not unduly bothered about the onward march of Socialism as long as it left them in power most of the time. Few of them seemed to realise that the institutional and economic bases were being laid which could fulfil Harold Wilson's dream and make Labour the permanent Party of Government on the Swedish model, which has already achieved forty years of Socialism. Mr Heath, as leader, was supposed to mark the breakaway from all this self-deception, but in office he seemed to have acquired all the high-minded paternalism and 'leadership' notions which his supporters thought they had thrown out—he even started talking about the unacceptable face of capitalism. So we had the unbalanced situation that Labour was behaving as a class party while the Tory leaders behaved as if they were above the struggle, despite their supporters' anguished cries. Mr Heath's overthrow, in retrospect, therefore looks far more inevitable than it did at the time.

Mrs Thatcher shares the gut feelings of her supporters more than her predecessor. She understands that the Tory Party's natural constituency is the social group which is most threatened by rapid inflation. Yet what a Party has to do is not merely to get out the vote: it must enthuse its supporters at least sufficiently to make some of them ready to go out canvassing. Sooner or later a Party has to stand for some idea if it is to survive. This may seem a surprising claim. The great Tory boast has long been that theirs is the Party of pragmatism, of action not words. And, indeed, Conservatives have held office for 18 out of the 30 years since the war broadly by two means. First, in order to gain power, by joining wholeheartedly in the business of promising to do better in spending the people's own money than the other side. Second, once in power, by manipulating the economy through the Keynesian economic management techniques mainly by creating booms before elections.

These pillars have now collapsed. The popular Tory image as the Party of prudent financial management has been severely damaged by leaving office twice running in the middle of a balance of payments crisis. As for Keynesian economic management, this has become the drug that now needs such large doses that if it is used any more it may kill the patient! Any further resort to the printing press to curb unemployment might cause runaway inflation. The bases of pragmatism have thus disappeared, and for that reason alone it is necessary to find an ideology. The other equally compelling reason is that Socialism has meantime made enormous gains in Britain. The share of the national income spent by the Government has risen more or less continuously since 1959, when it was 36 per cent until 1974 when it was over 54 per cent. This has meant that a rising proportion of employment is directly or indirectly dependent on the state; for not only do the numbers on the state and local authority payroll mount, but an increasing number of the contracts available to firms are coming from organisations that are state-owned or controlled. The number of people with a personal stake in the continuance or (for those with a career in Government Service) an extension of Socialism is now substantial, while nothing has grown faster than the amount of patronage at the disposal of the socialist councils. Further, many firms, since they have been required to publish details of political donations, have become reluctant to give money to the Conservative Party because they fear that ministries or Socialist-run local authorities will discriminate against them when it comes to placing orders or contracts. In all these circumstances pragmatism amounts to a policy of piecemeal surrender to socialism. Is that what Conservatives want?

The question is not a silly one. Conservatives have arrived at a point in their history where they must make up their minds about what sort of Party they wish to be. As Mr Michael Harrington argued in the spring issue of the excellent new journal *International Review*, Conservatives have a problem of identity. They cannot stand still. They must either join the trend to Socialism (which is arguably what pre-war Conservative Governments tended to do) and try to show that they are better at Socialist administration than the Socialists, or they must try to put Socialism into reverse. Does it matter? What is at stake? To resort to a much abused word, it is freedom. Concentration of power must mean beyond a certain point deprivation of freedoms we at present enjoy. For example, imagine if the state becomes the source of all employment: how easy it would be for anyone running a campaign against the Government to be shunted into an unsuitable job or, to have it made impossible to obtain a job at all! Or if all the media and means of communication are nationalised, all the studios, the newspapers, the publishing houses, the printing presses are state-owned, how easy it would be for the Government to prevent these facilities being made available to its opponents, or so infrequently available that their message is effectively suppressed!

Even if Labour were prepared to tolerate or even conceivably welcome them as an alternative Socialist Party, it is doubtful whether the Conservatives would prosper, for the policy has been tried already by the Conservatives in Scandinavia. The result—forty years of Socialists in power in Sweden, in Norway Conservative Parliamentary representation reduced to 5 per cent, and in Denmark to one-seventh of the Parliamentary seats. In Denmark indeed the Conservatives have less representation than the entirely new Party of Mr Mogens Glistrup, whose main platform is the abolition of Income Tax!

In fact, by choosing Mrs Thatcher the Conservatives have given a clear signal that the me-too response to Socialism is not for them. Self-reliance and personal independence have been her most consistent themes down the years, and she herself is a living and thriving example of what those qualities can achieve. She has a strong, almost Lockeian belief in property as the basis of personal freedom. She and Sir Keith Joseph have explicitly put their faith in the 'social market economy' as the alternative to Socialism. The phrase is Professor Erhardt's and the policy for which it stands provided the basis of the post-war German economic miracle. In essence it means the economy of free market capitalism for the strong, or at least the able-bodied, backed by a compassionate state which caters for the weak. The Government's role is otherwise seen as performing those functions—defence, maintaining law and order, administering justice, preserving a stable currency, and providing collective services (sewage, traffic control) which private enterprise cannot conveniently supply. The Welfare State as we have known it could ideally be replaced by a reverse Income Tax and a minimum income provision which would more effectively cater for the genuinely poor, but with far less bureaucracy.

What about the unions and the nationalised industries, the one an active threat to social and monetary stability, the other a roadblock in the path of progress, a sort of giant agency for the perpetuation of unproductive employment at the taxpayer's expense? As a matter of fact the Conservatives seem in retrospect to have made unduly heavy weather of the union question, partly because they allowed the policy to fall into the hands of the lawyers. The really important matter, as Mr Bernard Levin has recently sought to show in the case of the AEUW, is to prevent the minority of extremists from taking control by the institution of a postal ballot for vital elections, especially those for national affairs. If Conservative leaders were sincere, as they surely were, in professing their faith in the reasonableness of the rank and file of the union, then the one essential is to see that the rank and file are genuinely represented. Conservatives should also have a trade union organisation which deliberately and without apology joins in the union power struggle, instead of having such an organisation and then forbidding it to have anything to do with trade union elections. Pressure from Conservative trade unionists need not aim, at first anyway, at electing Conservatives, but, if the Communists, who could only produce 39,000 votes in the whole country in a General Election, can acquire a dominating position in the union movement in its present unreformed state, then surely the Conservatives with their far higher support among trade unionists could swing the balance in favour of the moderates!

Admittedly, even with a ballot reform there would be certain unions, like the miners, whose key position would enable them to hold the nation to ransom at certain times. There is nothing new about this. As Sir Geoffrey Howe is fond of pointing out, the miners were already holding the nation to ransom before (and indeed during) the Great War, when the mines were privately owned. Yet the conclusion to draw is not that we need some new pontifical organisation to pronounce on the justice of their case. Justice has little or nothing to do with it. The miners, like any other group, will grab more if they can. What makes them awkward is that they have unusual group solidarity and come from physically isolated and psychologically separate and self-sufficient communities, so that they are less swayed than the average by the pressures of public opinion. Thus, at those times when coal is in short supply, the result of the wage bargain is indeterminate. The community, however, will have to pay more, and somebody somewhere will have to exercise some political or diplomatic skill. Erecting an incomes policy around this situation is mainly an exercise in humbug and only makes things worse because it formalises and hastens confrontation, whereas what is wanted is as much fluidity and confusion over the issue as possible and the minimum of moral pronouncement. Meanwhile we had best, without too much fuss, get on with the business of minimising the market monopoly which recalcitrant groups of workers can exercise.

As regards the nationalised industries, the major problem is the defeatist conviction among the public and even among Conservative politicians that they cannot be unscrambled. Well they can, and details are given in *Goodbye to Nationalisation* (edited by Dr Rhodes Boyson, Churchill Press, 1971). One has only to instance Volkswagen, which sold in lots of two or three shares each, to over 1½ million shareholders. Shares could, in the last resort, even be given away to everybody on the electoral register—why should not the public own what is supposed to be publicly owned? Denationalisation could indeed be a main plank in the creation of the property-owning democracy which is Mrs Thatcher's ideal.

All this discourse is meant to indicate that the intellectual framework for the Thatcher approach to economy and society already exists. It is not a matter of having to formulate a new philosophy of policy, the material is already available. There is a whole library of studies on the application of market principles to the British economic situation, published by the Institute of Economic Affairs. What is needed is the magic touch, which Mrs Thatcher undoubtedly possesses, to make the move from dry-as-dust economics to the exciting prospect of a policy geared to creating a popular capitalism. It is a matter of vast good fortune for this country that when it faces what is probably an even more serious, because more insidious, danger than even at the time of Dunkirk, the Conservatives have a leader with a genuine alternative to Socialism which offers a real opportunity to restore prosperity, social harmony and national self-respect. The wide-spread enthusiasm which her election aroused was partly due to her novelty and partly to her striking looks, but more than all else, it was due to her being the embodiment of many hopes. Even in the jealous trade of politics it must be the near universal wish that she shall have the health, the strength and the opportunity to fulfil them.

INDEX